Ch

GW00739160

Korean phrasebook

Lucien Brown
Jaehoon Yeon

Chambers

First published by Chambers Harrap Publishers Ltd 2008
7 Hopetoun Crescent
Edinburgh EH7 4AY

ISBN 978 0550 10352 9

Publishing Manager
Anna Stevenson

Prepress
Helen Hucker
Becky Pickard

Designed and typeset by Chambers Harrap Publishers, Edinburgh
Printed and bound by Tien Wah Press (PTE.) LTD., Singapore
Illustrations: Art Explosion

CONTENTS

INTRODUCTION

This brand new English-Korean phrasebook from Chambers is ideal for anyone wishing to try out their foreign language skills while travelling abroad. The information is practical and clearly presented, helping you to overcome the language barrier and mix with the locals.

Each section features a list of useful words and a selection of common phrases: some of these you will read or hear, while others will help you to express yourself. The simple phonetic transcription system, specifically designed for English speakers, ensures that you will always make yourself understood.

The book also includes a mini bilingual dictionary of around 2500 words, so that more adventurous users can build on the basic structures and engage in more complex conversations.

Concise information on local culture and customs is provided, along with practical tips to save you time. After all, you're on holiday – time to relax and enjoy yourself! There is also a food and drink glossary to help you make sense of menus, and ensure that you don't miss out on any of the national or regional specialities.

Remember that any effort you make will be appreciated. So don't be shy – have a go!

ABBREVIATIONS USED IN THIS BOOK

adj	adjective
adv	adverb
n	noun
pl	plural
prep	preposition
sing	singular
v	verb

PRONUNCIATION

Korean script

The Korean alphabet consists of 40 characters. This alphabet is known as *Hangul* in South Korea and is commonly referred to by this name in English-language publications, including this phrasebook. However, it should be noted that in North Korea the alphabet is known by another name: *Chosŏngul*.

Unlike Chinese or Japanese script, the basics of Hangul take hours rather than weeks and months to learn. The pronunciation guides in this section include Korean script so that the more adventurous can have a go. However, be warned that pronunciation sometimes differs from spelling and that we don't go into all of these discrepancies here.

Don't worry if you don't learn any Hangul. The romanization provided in this book makes it easy for an English speaker to pronounce Korean very close to how it should sound.

Basic vowels

Korean has eight basic vowels:

Hangul	Pronunciation	Transcription
ㅏ	**a** as in **a**nt	a
ㅓ	**o** as in s**o**n	ŏ
ㅗ	**o** as in g**o**	o
ㅜ	**oo** as in b**oo**t	u
ㅣ	**ee** as in m**ee**t	i
ㅡ	**u** as in c**u**rt	ŭ
ㅐ	**a** as in c**a**re	ae
ㅔ	**e** as in p**e**n	e

Y-vowels

Y-vowels are combinations of the basic vowels and a "y" sound:

Hangul	Pronunciation	Transcription
ㅑ	**ya** as in **ya**p	ya
ㅕ	**you** as in **you**ng	yŏ

PRONUNCIATION

ㅛ	**yo** as in **yo**ga	*yo*
ㅠ	**yu** as in **yu**le	*yu*
ㅒ	**ye** as in **ye**sterday	*yeh*
ㅖ	**ye** as in **ye**sterday	*yeh*

W-vowels

W-vowels are formed by adding a w sound to the front of six of the basic vowels.

Hangul	Pronunciation	Transcription
ㅘ	**wa** as in **wa**g	*wa*
ㅝ	**wo** in **wo**rd	*wo*
ㅙ	**wea** as in **wea**r	*wae*
ㅞ	**we** as in **we**t	*we*
ㅚ	**we** as in **we**t	*we*
ㅟ	**wee** as in **wee**p	*wi*

Ui-vowel

There is one more complex vowel:

Hangul	Pronunciation	Transcription
ㅢ	**uey** as in chop s**uey** but a shorter sound	*ui*

Basic consonants

The Hangul script contains nine basic consonants. However, several of these have two distinct pronunciations. Unless otherwise indicated, the pronunciations are similar to those in English.

Hangul	Pronunciation	Transcription
ㄴ	**n** as in **n**o	*n*
ㅁ	**m** as in **m**op	*m*
ㄱ	**k** as in **k**ite, but softer, with no puff of air	*k*
	g as in **g**o	*g**

ㄷ	**t** as in **t**op, but softer, with no puff of air	t	
	d as in **d**og	d*	
ㅂ	**p** as in **p**int, but softer, with no puff of air	p	
	b as in **b**ull	b*	
ㅈ	**ch** as in **ch**air, but softer, with no puff of air	ch	
	j as in **j**am	j*	
ㄹ	rolled rather like the Spanish "r", with the tongue briefly touching the ridge behind the teeth	r	
	l as in **l**oop	l**	
ㅎ	**h** as in **h**ot	h	
ㅅ	**s** as in **s**ad	s	
	sh as in **sh**ip	sh***	
ㅇ	**ng** as in so**ng**	ng	

* These pronunciations only occur in the middle of a word, between two vowels.
** This pronunciation only occurs at the end of a word or when the character occurs twice together (ending one syllable and starting the next).
*** This pronunciation only occurs when the characters precedes the vowel *i*, any of the y-vowels or the w-vowel *wi*.

Aspirated consonants
These are all pronounced similar to the English equivalents, but followed by a stronger puff of air.

Hangul	Pronunciation	Transcription
ㅋ	**k** as in **k**ite but followed by a stronger puff of air	k'
ㅌ	**t** as in **t**o but followed by a stronger puff of air	t'

ㅍ	**p** as in **p**int but followed by a stronger puff of air	*p'*
ㅊ	**ch** as in **ch**air but followed by a stronger puff of air	*ch'*

Reinforced consonants

These are pronounced in roughly the same way as their English equivalents (k as in kite and so on), but much more forcefully, with the lips and tongues kept very tense.

Hangul	Transcription
ㄲ	*kk*
ㄸ	*tt*
ㅃ	*pp*
ㅆ	*ss*
ㅉ	*tch*

Stress

In most Korean words, the first syllable carries slightly more stress. Attempting to stress subsequent syllables is one of the most common pronunciation errors made by English speakers unfamiliar with Korean. When compared to English, the contrast between stressed and unstressed syllables is not so marked. The reason for this is that vowels *always* retain their original sounds. They are not reduced in the way they often are in unstressed syllables in English.

Intonation

Most statements in this phrasebook can be made into questions simply by adding a rising intonation, ie lifting your voice at the end of the statement.

More information on reading Hangul

Hangul letters are not written in a straight line but are clustered into syllable blocks. The word "Hangul", for example, is not as written ㅎㅏㄴㄱㅡㄹ (h-a-n-g-u-l) but as 한글 (han-gul).

The initial consonant is written to the left of a vertically-shaped vowel and above a horizontally shaped vowel:

가　　　고

거　　　구

When a syllable has a final consonant, this is written under the vowel:

간　　　군

Although some syllables have two final consonants, often only one is pronounced.

닭 (chicken) is pronounced *tak* and not *talk*.

When a syllable has no initial consonant sound, the circular ㅇ (otherwise pronounced *ng*) is written in this position but not pronounced. This creates no confusion because the *ng* sound can only occur at the end of a syllable:

용 (dragon) is pronounced *yong*

A note on romanization

In this book, we use a specially modified version of the McCune-Reischauer system to transliterate Korean words. However, this script may vary from romanizations you might encounter in South Korea. Since 2000, the South Korean government has been in the process of replacing McCune-Reischauer with a new system that can now be seen on most official signs throughout the country. Although this system is in some ways more logical, it tends to result in English speakers making more rather than fewer pronunciation errors! In this book, we only use this system in the romanization of place names.

A basic understanding of Korean etiquette and social behaviour can help make sure things go smoothly during your trip to Korea.

The most common form of greeting in Korea is bowing. A short dip of the head is normally sufficient; however, a deeper bow may be needed when meeting elders or superiors. Men will often shake hands; the handshake is often long and limp rather than firm and brisk and should be initiated by the elder or superior party. Kissing and hugging are not common forms of greeting or considered to be appropriate behaviour in public places.

When you visit someone's house, make sure you always take your shoes off at the door. It is common to bring a small gift, especially if you are visiting for the first time. Koreans often give food or drink, with fruit being particularly popular.

When eating and drinking with Koreans, always wait for the eldest or most senior person to start eating before you dig in. Koreans like to pour alcoholic drinks for each other. When doing this, make sure that you hold the bottle or glass with both hands when pouring or receiving fill-ups from superiors or people you are drinking with for the first time. Do not leave chopsticks sticking up in the rice; it is best to place spoons and chopsticks on the table when not eating.

The Korean language has a highly developed system of honorific forms used to address elders and superiors. As this kind of language is also used with strangers, phrases in this book already contain honorific forms where appropriate.

Generally speaking, Koreans do *not* address elders and superiors by name or with a pronoun such as "you" (although they will do so when using English). Instead, they will use another title or term of address. If you are unsure how to address an elder or superior, try using 선생님 *sŏnsaengnim*, which literally means "teacher" but can be used as a term of respect to more or less anyone.

When you are addressing people of similar or younger age, names are OK. To make it a little more polite, you can attach -씨 *-ssi* to their first name (eg Su-jin-*ssi*).

There are also several different terms of address you can use to attract the attention of people working in the service industry, such as waiters and taxi drivers. As long as they are over forty or so, females will answer to calls of 아줌마 *ajumma* (literally meaning "aunt") and males to 아저씨 *ajŏssi* ("uncle"). Note, however, that these terms are typically only used to blue-collar workers. When addressing younger or more upwardly mobile workers, things can be a little more complicated. The safest way is just to attract their attention with a shout of 여기요 *yŏgiyo* "over here". As well as using honorific language, showing general respect to elders and superiors is important in Korean culture. This includes trying not to contradict or disagree with them or causing them any embarrassment or loss of face.

Korean does not have different forms of greeting for different times of day such as "good morning", "good afternoon" and "good evening". Note, however, that there are different expressions depending on who is staying or leaving.

Korean also does not have a single word that translates as "please". Instead, the meaning of "please" is implied in expressions such as ⋯주 세요 … *chuseyo* ("I'd like …") – the most common polite way to ask for something in Korean.

The basics

excuse me 실례합니다 *shillehamnida*

goodbye *(said by person leaving to person staying)* 안녕 히 계세요 *annyŏnghi keseyo*; *(said by person leaving to person leaving or by both persons when both are on the move)* 안녕히 가세요 *annyŏngh kaseyo*

goodnight	*(when going to bed)* 안녕히 주무세요 *annyŏnghi chumuseyo*
hello	안녕하세요 *annyŏnghaseyo*
no	아니요 *aniyo*
OK	괜찮아요 *kwaench'anayo*, 오케이 *ok'ei*
pardon	미안합니다 *mianhamnida*
pardon?	네? *ney?*
thanks, thank you	감사합니다 *kamsahamnida*, 고맙습니다 *komapsŭmnida*
yes	네 *ne*, 예 *ye*

Expressing yourself

I'd like ...
… 주세요
… *chuseyo*

we'd like ...
… 주세요
… *chuseyo*

do you want ...?
… 좋으세요?
… *choŭseyo?*

do you have ...?
… 있어요?
… *issŏyo?*

is there a ...?
… 있어요?
… *issŏyo?*

are there any ...?
… 있어요?
… *issŏyo?*

how ...?
어떻게 …?
ŏttŏk'e …?

why ...?
왜 …?
wae …?

when ...?
언제 …?
ŏnje …?

what ...?
뭐 …?
mŏ …?

which ...?
무슨 …?
musŭn …?

where is/are ...?
… 어디에요?
… *ŏdi-eyo?*

how much is it?
얼마에요?
ŏlma-eyo?

what is it?
뭐에요?
mŏ-eyo?

EVERYDAY CONVERSATION

do you speak English?
영어 하세요?
yŏngŏ haseyo?

where are the toilets, please?
실례지만, 화장실 어디에요?
sillejiman, hwajangshil ŏdi-eyo?

how are you?
잘 지내셨어요?
chal chinaeshyŏssŏyo?

fine, thanks
네, 잘 지냈어요
ney, chal chinaessŏyo

no, thanks
아니오, 괜찮아요
anio, kwaench'anayo

yes, please
네, 좋습니다
ney, chosŭmnida

you're welcome
괜찮아요
kwaench'anayo

see you later
또 뵙겠습니다
tto pekessŭmnida

I'm sorry
죄송합니다
chwesonghamnida

Understanding

주의 *chuui*	attention
… 하지 마세요 *… haji maseyo*	do not …
… 금지 *… kumji*	do not…
입구 *ipku*	entrance
출구 *ch'ulgu*	exit
무료 *muryo*	free
주차금지 *chuch'agŭmji*	no parking
금연 *kŭmyŏn*	no smoking
영업중 *yŏngŏpchung*	open
닫힘 *tach'im*	closed
폐업 *p'eŏp*	closed
고장 *kojang*	out of order
예약석 *yeyaksŏk*	reserved
화장실 *hwajangshil*	toilets

··· 있어요
... *issŏyo*
there's/there are ...

···없어요
... *ŏpsŏyo*
there isn't/there aren't ...

어서 오세요
ŏsŏ oseyo
welcome

··· 해도 괜찮아요?
... *hae-do kwaench'anayo?*
do you mind if ...?

잠깐 기다리세요
chamkkan kidariseyo
one moment, please

앉으세요
anjŭseyo
please take a seat

PROBLEMS UNDERSTANDING KOREAN

Expressing yourself

pardon?
네?
ney?

what?
뭐라구요?
mŏraguyo?

could you repeat that, please?
다시 한번 말씀해 주세요
tashi hanbŏn malssŭmhae chuseyo

could you speak more slowly?
더 천천히 말씀해 주세요
tŏ ch'ŏnch'ŏnhi malssŭmhae chuseyo

I don't understand
잘 모르겠어요
chal morŭgessŏyo

I understand a little Korean
한국말 조금밖에 못 해요
hanggungmal chogum-ppakke mot haeyo

I can understand Korean but I can't speak it
한국말 알아듣지만 말 못 해요
hanggungmal aradutchiman mal mot haeyo

I hardly speak any Korean
한국말 거의 못 해요
hanggungmal kŏi mot haeyo

do you speak English?
영어 하세요?
yŏngŏ haseyo?

how do you spell it?
어떻게 써요?
ŏttŏke ssŏyo?

how do you say ... in Korean?
한국말로 … 뭐라고 해요?
hanggungmal-lo mŏrago haeyo?

what's that called in Korean?
그거 한국말로 뭐라고 해요?
kugŏ hanggungmal-lo mŏrago haeyo?

could you write it down for me?
써 주세요
ssŏ chuseyo

Understanding

한국말 하세요?
hanggungmal haseyo?
do you understand Korean?

… 라는 뜻이에요
… ranŭn ttush-ieyo
it means ...

써 드릴게요/써 줄게요
ssŏ tŭrilgeyo/ssŏ chulgeyo
I'll write it down for you

일종의 … 에요
iljong-e … -eyo
it's a kind of ...

SPEAKING ABOUT THE LANGUAGE

Expressing yourself

I learned a few words from my phrasebook
이 책에서 조금 배웠어요
i ch'aek-esŏ chogŭm paewossŏyo

I can just about get by
그냥 조금 알아요
kŭnyang chogŭm arayo

I hardly know two words!
잘 몰라요
chal mollayo

I find Korean a difficult language
한국말 어려워요
hanggungmal ŏryŏwoyo

I know the basics but no more than that
기초만 조금 알아요
kich'o-man chogŭm arayo

people speak too quickly for me
사람들이 너무 빨리 말해요
saram-dŭri nŏmu ppalli malhaeyo

Understanding

발음이 좋아요
parŭm-i choayo
you have a good accent

한국말 잘 하시네요
hanggungmal chal hashineyo
you speak very good Korean

ASKING THE WAY

Expressing yourself

excuse me, can you tell me where the ... is, please?
실례지만, … 어디에요?
sillejiman, … ŏdi-eyo?

which way is it to ...?
… 가는 길이 어디에요?
… ka-nŭn kil-i ŏdi-eyo?

can you tell me how to get to ...?
… 에 어떻게 가요?
… -e ŏttŏk'e kayo?

is there a ... near here?
이 근처에 … 있어요?
i kŭnch'ŏ-e … issŏyo?

I'm looking for ...
… 찾고 있는데요
… chakko innundeyo

could you show me on the map?
지도에서 가르쳐 주세요
chido-esŏ karŭch'yŏ chuseyo

is there a map of the town somewhere?
시내 지도 어디 있어요?
shinae chido ŏdi issŏyo?

is it far?
멀어요?
mŏroyo?

I'm lost
길을 잃었어요
kil-ul irŏssŏyo

Understanding

따라 가세요	*ttara kaseyo*	follow
내려 가세요	*naeryŏ kaseyo*	go down
올라 가세요	*olla kaseyo*	go up
계속 가세요	*kesok kaseyo*	keep going
왼쪽	*wentchok*	left
좌측	*chwach'ŭk*	left
오른쪽	*orŭntchok*	right
우측	*uch'ŭk*	right
곧장	*kotchang*	straight ahead
똑바로	*ttokparo*	straight ahead
돌아가세요	*toragaseyo*	turn

걸어가세요?
kŏrŏgaseyo?
are you on foot?

자동차로 오 분 걸려요
chadongch'a-ro o pun kŏllyŏyo
it's five minutes away by car

왼쪽 첫번째/두번째/세번째 길에 있어요
wentchok ch'ŏp-pŏntchae/tu-pŏntchae/se-pŏntchae kil-e issŏyo
it's the first/second/third on the left

교차로에서 오른쪽으로 가세요
kyoch'aro-esŏ orŭntchok-ŭro kaseyo
turn right at the intersection

은행에서 왼쪽으로 가세요
ŭnhaeng-esŏ wentchok-ŭro kaseyo
turn left at the bank

어 다음 출구에서 나가세요
i taŭm ch'ulgu-esŏ nagaseyo
take the next exit

멀지 않아요
mŏlji anayo
it's not far

바로 골목 근처에요
paro kolmok kŭnch'ŏ-eyo
it's just round the corner

GETTING TO KNOW PEOPLE

The basics

bad	나빠요 *nappayo*
beautiful	예뻐요 *yeppŏyo*, 아름다워요 *arŭmdawoyo*
boring	재미없어요 *chaemi-ŏpsŏyo*
cheap	싸요 *ssayo*
expensive	비싸요 *pissayo*
good	좋아요 *choayo*
great	아주 좋아요 *aju choayo*, 훌륭해요 *hullyunghaeyo*
interesting	재미있어요 *chaemi-issŏyo*
nice	멋있어요 *mŏsh-issŏyo*
not bad	나쁘지 않아요 *nappuji anayo*, 괜찮아요 *kwaench'anayo*
well	잘 *chal*
to hate	싫어해요 *sirŏhaeyo*
to like	좋아해요 *choahaeyo*
to love	사랑해요 *saranghaeyo*

INTRODUCING YOURSELF AND FINDING OUT ABOUT OTHER PEOPLE

Expressing yourself

my name's ...
제 이름은 … 이에요
che irŭm-ŭn ... i-eyo

what's your name?
이름이 뭐에요? *(to someone obviously younger)*
irŭm-i mŏ-eyo?
이름이 어떻게 되세요? *(to someone of similar age)*
irŭm-i ŏttŏk'e tweseyo?

성함이 어떻게 되세요? *(to someone significantly older)*
sŏngham-i ŏttŏk'e tweseyo?

how do you do!
처음 뵙겠습니다
chŏŭm pekkessumnida

pleased to meet you!
만나서 반갑습니다
mannasŏ pangapsumnida

this is my husband/my wife
우리 남편／집사람입니다
uri nampy'ŏn/chip saram-imnida

this is my partner, Karen
제 파트너 카렌입니다
ey p'at'ŭnŏ karen-imnidac

I'm English
(저는) 영국 사람이에요
(chŏ-nŭn) yŏngguk saram-ieyo

we're American
(우리는) 미국 사람이에요
(uri-nŭn) miguk saram-ieyo

I'm from ...
… 에서 왔어요
... esŏ wassŏyo

where are you from?
어느 나라 사람이세요?
ŏnŭ nara saram-iseyo?

how old are you?
몇 살이에요? *(to someone obviously younger)*
myŏt sal-ieyo
나이가 어떻게 되세요? *(to someone of similar age)*
nai-ga ŏttŏk'e tweseyo?
연세가 어떻게 되세요? *(to someone significantly older)*
yŏnse-ga ŏttŏk'e tweseyo?

I'm 22
스물 두 살이에요
sŭmul tu sal-ieyo

what do you do for a living?
직업이 뭐에요?／무슨 일을 하세요?
chigop-i mŏ-eyo?/musŭn il-ŭl haseyo?

are you a student?
학생이세요?
haksaeng-iseyo?

I work
일해요
ilhaeyo

I'm studying law
법률 공부하고 있어요
pŏmnyul kongbuhago issŏyo

I'm a teacher
선생이에요
sŏnsaeng-ieyo

GETTING TO
KNOW PEOPLE

19

I stay at home with the children
애들하고 집에 있어요
ae-dŭl-hago chip-e issŏyo

I work part-time
파트타임으로 일해요
p'at'ŭt'aim-ŭro ilhaeyo

I work in marketing
마케팅 분야에서 일해요
mak'et'ing punya-esŏ ilhaeyo

I'm retired
은퇴했어요
ŭnt'wehaessŏyo

I'm self-employed
자영업자에요
chayŏngŏpcha-eyo

I have two children
아이가 둘 있어요
ai-ga tul issŏyo

we don't have any children
아이가 없어요
ai-ga ŏpsŏyo

two boys and a girl
아들 둘하고 딸 하나
adŭl tul-hago ttal hana

a boy of five and a girl of two
다섯살 짜리 아들하고 두 살짜리 딸
tasŏt-sal tchari adŭl-hago tu sal-tchari ttal

have you ever been to Britain?
영국에 가본 적이 있어요?
yŏngguk-e ka-bon chŏk-i issŏyo?

Understanding

영국 사람이세요?
yŏngguk saram-iseyo?
are you English?

영국 잘 알아요
yŏngguk chal arayo
I know England quite well

우리도 여기 휴가 왔어요
uri-do yŏgi hyuga wassŏyo
we're on holiday here too

스코틀랜드에 한 번 가보고 싶어요
sŭk'ot'ŭllaendŭ-e han pŏn ka-bogo ship'ŏyo
I'd love to go to Scotland one day

TALKING ABOUT YOUR STAY

Expressing yourself

I'm here on business
사업때문에 여기 왔어요
saŏp-ttaemun-e yŏgi wassŏyo

I arrived three days ago
삼 일 전에 도착했어요
sam il chŏn-e toch'ak'aessŏyo

I'm only here for a long weekend
주말 연휴 동안만 여기 있을 거에요
chumal yŏnhyu tongan-man yŏgi issŭl kŏ-eyo

we're just passing through
그냥 지나가는 길이에요
kŭnyang chinaganŭn kil-ieyo

this is our first time in Korea
한국에 처음이에요
hangguk-e chŏŭm-ieyo

we're here to celebrate our wedding anniversary
결혼기념일을 축하하러 왔어요
kyŏron kinyŏmil-ŭl ch'uk' aharŏ wassŏyo

we're on our honeymoon
신혼여행 중이에요
shinhonyŏhaeng chung-ieyo

we're touring around
여기저기 여행하고 있어요
yŏgijŏgi yŏhaenghago issŏyo

we're on holiday
휴가로 왔어요
hyuga-ro wassŏyo

we've been here for a week
일주일동안 있었어요
il-chuil-tongan issŏssŏyo

we're here with friends
친구하고 같이 왔어요
ch'ingu-hago kach'i wassŏyo

GETTING TO KNOW PEOPLE

Understanding

재미있게 놀다 가세요
chaemi-ikke nolda kaseyo
enjoy your stay!

휴가 재미있게 보내세요
hyuga chaemi-ikke ponaeseyo
enjoy the rest of your holiday!

21

한국에 처음이세요?
hangguk-e ch'ŏŭm-iseyo?
is this your first time in Korea?

여기 좋아요?
yŏgi choayo?
do you like it here?

얼마나 계실 거에요?
ŏlmana keshil kŏeyo?
how long are you staying?

…에 가보셨어요?
....-e ka-boshyŏssŏyo?
have you been to …?

STAYING IN TOUCH

Expressing yourself

we should stay in touch
앞으로 서로 연락해요
ap'-ŭro sŏro yŏllak'eyo

I'll give you my e-mail address
제 이메일 주소 드릴게요
ce imeil chuso tŭrilkeyo

here's my address – get in touch if you ever come to Britain
여기 제 주소 있어요. 영국에 오시면 연락하세요
yŏgi che chuso issŏyo. yŏngguk-e o-shimyŏn yŏllak'aseyo

Understanding

주소 좀 가르쳐 주시겠어요?
chuso chom karŭch'yŏ chushigessŏyo?
will you give me your address?

이메일 주소 있으세요?
imeil chuso issŭseyo?
do you have an e-mail address?

언제든지 저희 집에 오셔서 묵으셔도 돼요
ŏnjedŭnji chŏ-ui chip-e oshyŏsŏ mugŭshyŏ-do twaeyo
you're always welcome to come and stay with us here

EXPRESSING YOUR OPINION

Some informal expressions

최고예요! *chwego-eyo!* it's the best!
그저 그래요 *kŭjŏ kŭraeyo* it's just so-so
별로예요 *pyŏllo-eyo* it's not so good
꽝이에요 *kkwang-ieyo* it's the pits!

Expressing yourself

I really like ...
··· 정말 좋아요
... chŏngmal choayo

I really liked ...
··· 정말 좋았어요
... chŏngmal choassŏyo

I don't like ...
··· 좋아하지 않아요
... choahaji anayo

I didn't like ...
··· 좋아하지 않았어요
... choahaji anassŏyo

I love ...
··· 아주 좋아해요
... aju choahaeyo

I loved ...
··· 아주 좋아했어요
... aju choahaessŏyo

I would like ...
··· 하고 싶어요
... -hago ship'ŏyo

I would have liked ...
··· 하고 싶었어요
... -hago ship'ŏssŏyo

I find it ...
··· (다/라)고 생각해요
... -(ta/ra)go saenggak'aeyo

I found it ...
··· (다/라)고 생각했어요
... -(ta/ra)go saenggak'aessŏyo

it's lovely
좋아요
choayo

it was lovely
좋았어요
choassŏyo

I agree
저도 그렇게 생각해요
chŏ-do kŭrŏk'e saenggak'aeyo

I don't agree
저는 그렇게 생각 안 해요
chŏ-nŭn kŭrŏk'e saenggak an haeyo

I don't know
잘 모르겠어요
chal morŭgessŏyo

I don't mind
상관없어요
sanggwan-ŏpsŏyo

I don't like the sound of it
저는 별로에요
chŏ-nun pyŏllo-eyo

it really annoys me
정말 싫어요
chŏngmal shirŏyo

it's a rip-off
바가지에요
pagaji-eyo

it's too busy
너무 복잡해요
nŏmu pokchap'aeyo

I really enjoyed myself
정말 재미있었어요
chŏngmal chaemi-issŏssŏyo

it sounds interesting
재미있을 거 같아요
chaemi-issŭl kŏ kat'ayo

it was boring
재미없어요
chaemi-ŏpsŏyo

it gets very busy at night
밤에는 정말 복잡해요
pam-e-nŭn chŏngmal pokchap'aeyo

it's very quiet
아주 조용해요
aju choyonghaeyo

we had a great time
정말 즐거웠어요
chŏngmal chŭlgŏwossŏyo

there was a really good atmosphere
분위기가 아주 좋았어요
punwigi-ga aju choassŏyo

we met some nice people
아주 좋은 사람들을 만났어요
aju choŭn saram-dŭl-ŭl mannassŏyo

we found a great hotel
아주 좋은 호텔을 찾았어요
aju choŭn hot'el-ŭl ch'ajassŏyo

Understanding

… 좋아하세요?
… choahaseyo?
do you like …?

… 에 가 보세요
… -e ka poseyo
you should go to …

재미있었어요?
chaemi-issŏssŏyo?
did you enjoy yourselves?

… 추천합니다
… ch'uch'ŏnhamnida
I recommend …

아주 좋은 곳이에요
aju choŭn kosh-ieyo
it's a lovely area

관광객들이 많지 않아요
kwangwanggaek-dul-i manch'i anayo
there aren't too many tourists

주말에 가지 마세요. 너무 복잡해요
chumal-e kaji maseyo. nŏmu pokchap'aeyo
don't go at the weekend, it's too busy

좀 과대평가됐어요
chom kwadaep'yŏnggadwaessŏyo
it's a bit overrated

TALKING ABOUT THE WEATHER

Some informal expressions

사우나 같아요! *sauna kat'ayo!* it's boiling! (literally, it's like a sauna)
몸이 꽁꽁 얼어요! *mom-i kkong-kkong ŏlŏyo!* I'm frozen solid!
비가 쏟아져요! *pi-ga ssodajyŏyo!* it's pouring with rain!

Expressing yourself

have you seen the weather forecast for tomorrow?
내일 일기예보 보셨어요?
naeil ilgiyebo poshyŏssŏyo?

it's going to be nice
날씨가 좋을 거예요
nalshi-ga choŭl kŏ-eyo

it isn't going to be nice
날씨가 안 좋을 거예요
nalshi-ga an choŭl kŏ-eyo

it's really hot
정말 더워요
chŏngmal tŏwoyo

it gets cold at night
밤에는 추워져요
pam-e-nŭn ch'uwojyŏyo

the weather was beautiful
날씨가 좋았어요
nalshi-ga choassŏyo

it rained a few times
가끔 비가 왔어요
kakkŭm pi-ga wassŏyo

there was a thunderstorm
천둥이 쳤어요
ch'ŏndung-i ch'yŏssŏyo

it's been lovely all week
일주일 내내 날씨가 좋았어요
iljuil naenae nalssi-ga choassŏyo

it's very humid here
습기가 아주 많아요
sŭpki-ga aju manayo

we've been lucky with the weather
운좋게 날씨가 아주 좋았어요
unjok'e nalssi-ga aju choassŏyo

Understanding

비가 올 거에요
pi-ga ol kŏ-eyo
it's supposed to rain

이번 주에 날씨가 좋다고 했어요
ibŏn chu-e nalssi-ga chot'ago haessŏyo
they've forecast good weather for the rest of the week

내일도 아주 더울 거에요
naeil-do aju tŏul kŏ-eyo
it will be hot again tomorrow

TRAVELLING

The basics

airport	공항 konghang
boarding	탑승 t'apsŭng
boarding card	탑승권 t'apsŭnggwon, 탑승 카드 t'apsŭng k'adŭ
boat	배 pae, 선박 sŏnbak
bus	버스 pŏsŭ
bus station	버스 터미날 pŏsŭ tŏminal
bus stop	버스 정류장 pŏsŭ chŏngnyujang
car	자동차 chadongch'a
check-in	체크인 ch'ek'ŭ-in
coach	관광버스 kwangwang pŏsŭ, 고속버스 kosok pŏsŭ
ferry	페리 peri, 배 pae
flight	비행기 pihaenggi
gate	탑승구 t'apsŭnggu
left-luggage (office)	수하물 보관소 suhamul pogwanso
luggage	수하물 suhamul, 가방 kabang
map	지도 chido
motorway	고속도로 kosoktoro
passport	여권 yŏgwon
plane	비행기 pihaenggi
platform	플랫폼 p'ŭllaetp'om
railway station	기차역 kich'ayŏk
return (ticket)	왕복(표) wangbok(p'yo)
road	도로 toro, 길 kil
shuttle bus	셔틀버스 shyŏt'ŭl pŏsŭ
single (ticket)	편도(표) p'yŏndo(p'yo)
street	거리 kŏri, 길 kil
taxi	택시 t'aekshi
terminal	터미날 t'ŏminal
ticket	표 p'yo
timetable	시간표 shiganp'yo
town centre	시내 shinae
train	기차 kich'a

underground	지하철 *chihach'ŏl*
underground station	지하철 역 *chihach'ŏl yŏk*
to book	예약해요 *yeyak'aeyo*
to check in	체크인해요 *ch'ek'inhaeyo*
to hire	빌려요 *pillyŏyo*

Expressing yourself

where can I buy tickets?
표 어디서 팔아요?
p'yo ŏdisŏ p'alayo?

a ticket to …, please
… 가는 표 주세요
… kanŭn p'yo chuseyo

I'd like to book a ticket
표 예약하고 싶어요
p'yo yeyak'ago ship'ŏyo

how much is a ticket to …?
… 가는 표 얼마에요?
… kanŭn p'yo ŏlma-eyo?

are there any concessions for students?
학생 할인 있어요?
haksaeng halin issŏyo?

could I have a timetable, please?
시간표 주세요
shiganp'yo chuseyo

is there an earlier/a later one?
빠른/늦은 거 있어요?
pparŭn/nŭjŭn kŏ issŏyo?

how long does the journey take?
얼마나 걸려요?
ŏlmana kŏllyŏyo?

is this seat free?
이 자리 비었어요?
i chari piŏssŏyo?

I'm sorry, there's someone sitting there
아니요, 누가 있어요
aniyo, nuga issŏyo

Understanding

도착	*toch'ak*	arrivals
취소	*ch'wiso*	cancelled
연결	*yŏnggyŏl*	connections
출발	*chulbal*	departures
입구	*ipku*	entrance
출입금지	*chulipkŭmji*	no entry
안내	*annae*	information
연착	*yŏnch'ak*	delayed
출구	*ch'ulgu*	exit
화장실	*hwajangshil*	toilets
남자	*namja*	gents
여자	*yŏja*	ladies
항공권	*hanggonggwon*	tickets

만원
manwon
everything is fully booked

BY PLANE

Two airlines are based in South Korea: Korean Air (대한항공 *taehan hanggong*) and Asiana Airlines (아시아나 항공 *ashiana hanggong*). As well as international flights, these two carriers also fly domestically between fourteen cities in South Korea. Although more expensive than coach or train travel, ticket prices are reasonable and the service is reliable. When flying from Seoul, domestic flights depart from the more centrally located Gimpo airport, whereas almost all international flights depart from Incheon. The national carrier of North Korea is Air Koryo (고려 항공 *koryŏ hanggong*). The airline has a limited schedule of international flights and no regular domestic service.

Expressing yourself

where's the British Airways check-in?
브리티시 에어웨이(영국항공) 첵크인이 어디에요?
british airways (yŏngguk hanggong) ch'ek'ŭ-in-i ŏdi-eyo?

I've got an e-ticket
전자 티켓이 있어요
chŏnja tik'esh-i issŏyo

one suitcase and one piece of hand luggage
가방 하나하고 핸드 캐리 하나요
kabang hana-hago haendŭ k'aeri hana-yo

what time do we board?
탑승이 몇시에요?
t'apsŭng-i myŏshi-eyo?

I'd like to confirm my return flight
비행기 예약 확인하고 싶어요
pihaenggi yeyak hwaginhago ship'ŏyo

one of my suitcases is missing
가방이 없어졌어요
kabang-i ŏpsŏjyŏssŏyo

my luggage hasn't arrived
짐이 안 도착했어요
chim-i an toch'ak'aessŏyo

the plane was two hours late
비행기가 두 시간 연착했어요
pihaenggi-ga tu shigan yŏnch'ak'aessŏyo

I've missed my connection
연결편을 놓쳤어요
yŏngyŏl-p'yŏn-ŭl noch'yŏssŏyo

I've left something on the plane
물건을 비행기에 두고 내렸어요
mulgŏn-ŭl pihaenggi-e tugo naeryŏssŏyo

I want to report the loss of my luggage
수하물 분실 신고를 하고 싶어요
suhamul punshil shingo-rŭl hago ship'ŏyo

Understanding

수하물 수취대	suhamul such'widae	baggage reclaim
탑승수속	t'apsŭngsusok	check-in
세관	segwan	customs
라운지	raunji	departure lounge
국내선	kuknaesŏn	domestic flights
면세	myŏnse	duty free
세관 신고	segwan shingo	goods to declare
탑승 진행중	t'apsŭng chinhaeng-jung	immediate boarding
신고할 물건 없음	shingohal mulgŏn ŏpsŭm	nothing to declare
입국 심사	ipkuk shimsa	passport control

출발 라운지에서 기다리세요
ch'ulbal raunji-esŏ kidariseyo
please wait in the departure lounge

창가가 좋으세요, 복도가 좋으세요?
ch'anga-ga choŭseyo, pokto-ga choŭseyo?
would you like a window seat or an aisle seat?

... 에서 갈아타세요
...-esŏ karat'aseyo
you'll have to change in …

가방은 몇 개에요?
kabang-ŭn myŏt kae-eyo?
how many bags do you have?

직접 짐을 싸셨어요?
chikchŏp chim-ŭl ssashyŏssŏyo?
did you pack all your bags yourself?

다른 사람의 짐은 없어요?
talŭn saram-e chim-ŭn ŏpsŏyo?
has anyone given you anything to take onboard?

무게가 5킬로그램 초과입니다
muge-ga o-k'illoguraem ch'ogwa-imnida
your luggage is five kilos overweight

여기 탑승권입니다
yŏgi t'apsŭnggwon-imnida
here's your boarding card

탑승은 … 에 시작입니다
t'apsŭng-ŭn … -e shijag-imnida
boarding will begin at …

탑승구 번호 … 로 가세요
t'apsŭngku pŏnho … -ro kaseyo
please proceed to gate number …

… 행 비행기 마지막 탑승 안내입니다
… haeng pihaenggi majimak t'apsŭng annae-imnida
this is a final call for …

가방이 도착했는지 이 번호로 전화해 보세요
kabang-i toch'ak'aennŭnji i pŏnho-ro chŏnhwahae poseyo
you can call this number to check if your luggage has arrived

BY TRAIN, COACH, BUS, UNDERGROUND, TRAM

South Korea has an efficient and affordable train and coach network connecting major towns and cities. Seoul is linked to Busan by the new super-fast KTX train service, which uses French-designed TGV trains. This new service has cut the journey time from the capital to the second city from 4 hours 10 minutes to 2 hours 40 minutes. Other classes of train include the 새마을호 *saemaul-ho* express service and the 무궁화호 *mugunghwa-ho* train. The latter stops at more stations and also allows standing passengers. Train tickets for weekend travel tend to sell out fast, so buying in advance is a wise move. Coach travel is also a good option for travelling around South Korea. Prices are cheaper than the train and the network is more extensive.

South Korea also has excellent local transportation facilities. Seoul, Busan and Taegu have clean, reliable and affordable underground systems as well as extensive networks of local buses. Seoul's underground system is particularly convenient to use as it covers the majority of the city and its suburbs and represents a fast and easy way to get about. Even if you are only going to be in Seoul a few days, it usually works out cheaper and easier to buy a pre-paid transport card (교통 카드 *kyot'ong k'adŭ*). These can be bought and topped up at all underground stations as well as local stores. With this card, you can also transfer between the underground and the local bus network (as well as between buses). The underground and now most buses have English/romanized signs.

As almost all travellers to North Korea will visit on an organized tour, you are more likely to be escorted around than be left to deal with public transport. Having said this, some tours do involve trips by train, including reaching P'yŏngyang by rail from Beijing. Also, some visitors to P'yŏngyang are allowed to use the underground system and check out the ornate station architecture. North Korean public transport also includes a system of trams: a mode of transport not seen in the South.

Expressing yourself

can I have a map of the underground, please?
지하철 노선도 있어요?
chihach'ŏl nosŏndo issŏyo?

what time is the next train to …?
… 행 다음 기차는 몇 시에요?
… haeng taŭm kich'a-nŭn myŏ shi-eyo?

what time is the last train?
마지막 기차는 몇 시에요?
majimak kich'a-nŭn myŏ shi-eyo?

which platform is it for …?
… 행 기차는 플랫폼 몇 번이에요?
… haeng kich'a-nŭn p'ŭllaetp'om myŏt pŏn-i-eyo?

where can I catch a bus to …?
… 가는 버스 어디서 타요?
… ka-nŭn pŏsŭ ŏdisŏ t'ayo?

does this bus/train go to …?
이 버스/기차 … 가요?
i pŏsŭ/kich'a … kayo?

which line do I take to get to …?
… 가려면 몇 호선 타야 돼요?
… karyŏmyŏn myŏt hosŏn t'aya twaeyo?

is this the stop for …?
여기가 … 에요?
yŏgi-ga … -eyo?

is this where the bus leaves for …?
여기서 … 가는 버스 출발해요?
yŏkisŏ … ka-nŭn pŏsŭ ch'ulbalhaeyo?

can you tell me when I need to get off?
어디서 내리는지 가르쳐 주세요
ŏdisŏ naerinŭnji karŭch'yŏ chuseyo

I've missed my train/bus
기차／버스를 놓쳤어요
kich'a/pŏsŭ-rŭl noch'yŏssŏyo

Understanding

기차 타는 곳 *kich'a t'anŭn kot*	to the trains
매표소 *maep'yoso*	ticket office
오늘(금일) 출발 *onŭl (kŭmil) ch'ulba*	tickets for travel today
일주일 *iljuil*	weekly
일개월 *ilgaewol*	monthly
오늘/당일/금일 *onul/tangil/kŭmil*	for the day
예약 *yeyak*	bookings

오른쪽으로 좀 더 가면 정류장어 있습니다
olŭntchok-uro chom tŏ kamyŏn chŏngnyujang-i issumnida
there's a stop a bit further along on the right

잔돈 없음
chandon ŏpsŭm
exact money only, please

… 에서 갈아타세요
… -esŏ kalat'aseyo
you'll have to change at …

… 번 버스를 타세요
… pŏn pŏsŭ-rŭl t'aseyo
you need to get the number … bus

34

이 기차는 … 에 정차합니다	여기서 두 정거장
i kich'a-nŭn … -e chŏngch'ahamnida	*yŏgisŏ tu chŏnggŏjang*
this train calls at …	two stops from here

BY CAR

With the inexpensive and highly developed public transport system in South Korea, driving may not represent the best option for getting about, particularly if you plan to stick to the major towns and cities. Traffic is also notoriously heavy both within the cities and on motorways. However, rural road networks are generally good and pleasant to drive around. You will need an International Driving Permit to drive in South Korea.

Taxis are inexpensive and generally easy to flag down in the major cities. The only time you may struggle to find one is after midnight, in the hour or so after the public transportation system shuts down for the night. At these times, taxi drivers will also try to pick up multiple fares from different passengers heading in similar directions. Drivers will slow down and listen for the shouts of potential passengers, calling out their intended destinations.

As well as normal taxis (which are silver-grey in Seoul and yellow in many provincial towns), there are also black deluxe taxis (모범 택시 *mobŏm t'aekshi*). These are plusher and more expensive and are not permitted to pick up multiple fares.

Hitchhiking is not a common practice in South Korea. In fact, if you stand by the roadside with your thumb out, don't expect everyone to know what you are doing! However, some visitors have got around the countryside by asking locals for lifts and have reported that drivers are generally helpful and friendly. Although there is nothing to suggest that this is particularly dangerous, hitching with a friend is always a good idea.

Expressing yourself

where can I find a service station?
주유소가 어디 있어요?
chuyuso-ga ŏdi issŏyo?

lead-free petrol, please
무연(으로) 부탁합니다
muyŏn(-ŭro) put'ak'amnida

how much is it per litre?
일 리터에 얼마에요?
il lit'ŏ-e ŏlma-eyo?

we got stuck in a traffic jam
교통이 막혔어요
kyot'ong-i mak'yŏssŏyo

is there a garage near here?
이 근처에 정비소 있어요?
i kŭnjŏ-e chŏngbiso issŏyo?

can you help us to push the car?
차 좀 밀어 주시겠어요?
ch'a chom milŏ chusigessŏyo?

the battery's dead
배터리가 나갔어요
paet'ŏri-ga nagassŏyo

I've broken down
고장 났어요
kojang nassŏyo

we've run out of petrol
기름이 떨어졌어요
kirŭm-i ttŏrŏjyŏssŏyo

I've got a puncture and my spare tyre is flat
(타이어가) 펑크 났어요. 스패어 타이어도 터졌어요
(taiŏ-ga) p'ŏngk'ŭ nassŏyo. sŭp'aeŏ t'aiŏ-do t'ŏjyŏssŏyo

we've just had an accident
사고가 났어요
sago-ga nassŏyo

I've lost my car keys
차 열쇠를 잃어버렸어요
cha yŏlswe-rul irŏbŏryŏssŏyo

how long will it take to repair?
고치는 데 얼마나 걸려요?
koch'inŭn te ŏlmana kŏllyŏyo?

◆ Hiring a car

I'd like to hire a car for a week
일주일동안 차를 빌리고 싶은데요
iljuil-dongan ch'a-rul pilligo ship'ŭndeyo

how much does it cost per day?
하루에 얼마에요?
halu-e ŏlma-eyo?

an automatic (car)
오토매틱 (자동차)
ot'omaet'ik (chadongch'a)

do I have to fill the tank up before I return it?
기름을 채워서 반납해야 돼요?
kirŭm-ŭl ch'aewosŏ pannaphaeya twae-yo?

I'd like to take out comprehensive insurance
종합보험을 들어 주세요
chonghap-pohŏm-ul tŭlŏ chuseyo

◆ **Getting a taxi**

is there a taxi rank near here?
이 근처에 택시 승차장 있어요?
i kŭnj'ŏ-e t'aekshi sŭngch'ajang issŏyo?

I'd like to go to …
… 에 가 주세요
… -e ka chuseyo

I'd like to book a taxi for 8pm
8시에 택시 보내 주세요
yŏdŏl-si-e t'aekshi ponae chuseyo

you can drop me off here, thanks
여기 내려 주세요. 감사합니다
yŏki naeryŏ chuseyo. kamsahamnida

how much will it be to go to the airport?
공항 가는 데 얼마에요?
konghang ka-nŭn te ŏlma-eyo?

◆ **Hitchhiking**

I'm going to …
… 에 가는데요
… -e kanŭndeyo

can you drop me off here?
여기 내려 주세요
yŏgi nayryŏ chuseyo

could you take me as far as ...?
··· 까지 태워 주세요
... -kkaji t'aewo chuseyo

thanks for the lift
태워 주셔서 감사합니다
t'aewo chushyŏsŏ kamsamnida

we hitched a lift
히치하이크해서 왔어요
hich'ihaik'ŭ-haesŏ wassŏyo

Understanding

다른 방향 tarŭn panghyang	other directions
만원 manwon	full (car park)
자리 없음 chari ŏpsŭm	full (car park)
자리 있음 chari issŭm	spaces (car park)
티켓을 보관하세요 tik'es-ŭl pogwanhaseyo	keep your ticket
자동차 렌트 chadongch'a rentŭ	car hire
렌트카 rentŭ-k'a	car hire
주차장 chuch'ajang	car park
천천히 ch'ŏnch'ŏnhi	slow
서행 sŏhaeng	slow
주차금지 chuch'agŭmchi	no parking
주차엄금 chuch'a-ŏmgŭm	no parking
모든 방향 modŭn panghyang	all directions
제한 속도 chehan sokto	speed limit
주행차선 chuhaengch'asŏn	get in lane

운전면허증하고 여권하고 신용카드 좀 보여주세요
unjŏnmyŏnhŏjŭng-hago yŏgwon-hago shinyongk'adŭ chom poyŏ chuseyo
I'll need your driving licence, passport and credit card

보증금은 십만원입니다
pojŭnggŭm-ŭn simman-won-imnida
there's a 100,000-won deposit

좋아요, 타세요. …까지 모셔다 드릴게요
choayo, t'aseyo. …-kkachi mosyŏda tŭrilgeyo
all right, get in, I'll take you as far as …

BY BOAT

South Korea has an extensive ferry service connecting the mainland to offshore islands. Destinations include Jejudo to the south, Ulleungdo to the east and numerous small islands off the south and west coasts. There are also ferry services linking the southern city of Busan with Japan. From Incheon (to the west of Seoul), you can catch ferries to the east coast of China.

Expressing yourself

how long is the crossing?
항해 시간은 얼마나 걸려요?
hanghay sigan-ŭn ŏlmana kŏllyŏyo?

I feel seasick
배멀미를 해요
paemŏlmi-rŭl haeyo

Understanding

보행자/자동차 없는 승객
pohaengja/chadongch'a ŏm-nun sŭngkaek
foot passengers only

다음 배편/출발은 … 입니다
taŭm paep'yŏn/ch'ulbal-ŭn … imnida
the next crossing is at …

South Korea offers a variety of accommodation options to suit travellers on all budgets.

Although Korean also uses the word "hotel" (호텔 *hot'el*), this is reserved for Western-style accommodation. The range of hotels and the accommodation they offer is roughly equivalent to what you will find in the West. Prices for a double or twin room may range from around 50,000 up to 300,000 won per night. The word "motel" (모텔 *mot'el*) has quite different connotations in Korea than in the West. These are cheap hotels with small rooms that are often used as "love hotels". However, it is quite acceptable to treat such establishments just as a cheap form of accommodation. If you can put up with the frilly decor, they represent a decent option for budget travellers. *Yŏgwan* (여관) are Korean-style inns, often with shared bathroom facilities. Most rooms are of the traditional Korean 온돌 *ondol* style – you sleep on a blanket on a heated floor rather than on a bed. *Yŏgwan* are generally cheaper than Western-style hotels. *Minbak* (민박), sometimes referred to in English as "homestays", are rooms in private houses. Bathroom and kitchen facilities are often shared with the family – meals can usually be provided on request. If you are planning to stay in more remote villages, this may be the only accommodation option available.

South Korea only has a handful of youth hostels, but most are modern with good facilities. If you are looking for something totally different, several Buddhist temples now offer accommodation and fascinating insights into Korean culture.

Visitors to North Korea are only permitted to stay in designated hotels. These are modern hotels purpose-built for foreign tourists.

The basics

apartment   아파트 *ap'at'ŭ*
bath   욕조 *yokcho*

bathroom	욕실 *yokshil*
bathroom with shower	샤워 딸린 욕실 *shyawo ttallin yokshil*
bed	침대 *ch'imdae*
bed and breakfast	조식 포함 *choshik p'oham*
cable television	케이블 티비 *k'eibŭl t'ibi*
campsite	캠핑장 *k'aemp'ingjang*
caravan	캬라반 *k'yaraban*
double bed	더블 침대 *tŏbŭl ch'imdae*
double room	이인실 *i-inshil*
en-suite bathroom	욕실 완비 *yokshil wambi*
family room	가족실 *kajokshil*
flat	아파트 *ap'at'ŭ*
full-board	삼식 제공 *samshik chegong*
fully inclusive	전체 포함 *chŏnch'e p'oham*
half-board	아침 저녁 제공 *ach'im chŏnyŏk chegong*
hotel	호텔 *hot'el*
key	열쇠 *yŏlswe*
rent	렌트 *rentŭ*
self-catering	자취 *chach'wi*
shower	샤워 *shyawo*
single bed	싱글 침대 *singŭl ch'imdae*
single room	일인실 *il-inshil*
tenant	세입자 *seipcha*
tent	텐트 *t'ent'ŭ*
toilets	화장실 *hwajangshil*
youth hostel	유스호스텔 *yusŭhosŭt'el*
to book	예약해요 *yeyak'aeyo*
to rent	렌트해요 *rentŭ-haeyo*
to reserve	예약해요 *yeyak'aeyo*

ACCOMMODATION

Expressing yourself

I have a reservation
예약했는데요
yeyak'aennŭndeyo

the name's …
이름은 … 이에요
irŭm-ŭn … -ieyo

do you take credit cards?
신용카드 받아요?
shinyong-k'adŭ padayo?

where do we leave the keys?
열쇠는 어디서 반환해요?
yŏlswe-nŭn ŏdisŏ panhwanhaeyo?

are bed linen and towels provided?
침대 시트하고 수건 있어요?
ch'imdae shit'ŭ-hago sukkŏn issŏyo?

is a car necessary?
자동차가 필요해요?
chadongch'a-ga p'iryohaeyo?

is the accommodation suitable for elderly people?
노인이 살기에 편해요?
noin-i salgi-e p'yŏnhaeyo?

where is the nearest supermarket?
가까운 슈퍼(마켓)은 어디 있어요?
kakkaun sup'ŏ(mak'et)-ŭn ŏdi issŏyo?

Understanding

빈방 있음 *pinbang issŭm*	vacancies
만원 *manwon*	full
출입금지 *ch'ulipkumji*	private
카운터 *k'aunt'ŏ*	reception
화장실 *hwajangshil*	toilets

여권 좀 보여 주시겠어요?
yŏgwon chom poyŏ chusigessŏyo?
could I see your passport, please?

이 서류 좀 작성해 주세요
i sŏryu chom chaksŏnghae chuseyo
could you fill in this form?

HOTELS

Expressing yourself

do you have any vacancies?
빈 방 있어요?
pin pang issŏyo?

for three nights
삼 박
sam pak

how much is a double room per night?
이인실 하루에 얼마에요?
i-inshil haru-e ŏlma-eyo?

I'd like to reserve a double room/a single room
일인실／이인실 예약하고 싶어요
il-inshil/ i-inshil yeyak'ago ship'ŏyo

would it be possible to stay an extra night?
일 박 더 할 수 있어요?
il pak tŏ hal su issŏyo?

do you have any rooms available for tonight?
오늘 밤 빈 방 있어요?
onŭl pam pin pang issŏyo?

do you have any family rooms?
가족실 있어요?
kajokshil issŏyo?

would it be possible to add an extra bed?
침대 하나 더 줄 수 있어요?
ch'imdae hana tŏ chul su issŏyo?

could I see the room first?
방 좀 볼 수 있어요?
pang chom pol su issŏyo?

do you have anything bigger/quieter?
더 큰／조용한 방 있어요?
tŏ k'ŭn/choyonghan pang issŏyo?

that's fine, I'll take it
좋아요. 이 걸로 주세요
choayo, i kŏl-lo chuseyo

could you recommend any other hotels?
다른 호텔 좀 소개해 주세요
tarŭn hot'el chom sogaehae chuseyo

is breakfast included?
아침 식사 포함이에요?
ach'im shiksa p'oham-ieyo?

what time do you serve breakfast?
아침 식사는 몇 시에요?
ach'im shiksa-nŭn myŏ shi-eyo?

is there a lift?
엘리베이터 있어요?
ellibeit'ŏ issŏyo?

is the hotel near the centre of town?
호텔이 시내 가까이 있어요?
hot'el-i shinae kakkai issŏyo?

what time will the room be ready?
몇 시에 방에 들어갈 수 있어요?
myŏ shi-e pang-e tŭrŏkal su issŏyo?

the key for room ..., please
··· 번 방 열쇠 주세요
... pŏn pang yŏlswe chuseyo

could I have an extra blanket?
이불 하나 더 주세요
ibul hana tŏ chuseyo

the air conditioning isn't working
에어콘이 안 나와요
eŏk'on-i an nawayo

could I book a wake-up call, please?
모닝콜 좀 해 주세요
moningk'ol chom hae chuseyo

I'd like to check out, please
체크 아웃 해 주세요
ch'ek'ŭ aut hae chuseyo

Understanding

죄송하지만 방이 없습니다
chwesonghajiman pang-i ŏpssŭmnida
I'm sorry, but we're full

일인실 밖에 없어요
ilinshil pakk-e ŏpssŏyo
we only have a single room available

몇 박이에요?
myŏt pak-ieyo?
how many nights is it for?

성함이 어떻게 되세요?
sŏngham-i ŏttŏk'e tweseyo?
what's your name, please?

체크 인은 열 두 시부터입니다
ch'ekk'ŭ in-ŭn yŏl tu shi-put'ŏ-imnida
check-in is from midday

오전 열 한시 이전에 체크 아웃하셔야 합니다
ojŏn yŏl han-shi ijŏn-e ch'ek'ŭ aut-hashyŏya hamnida
you have to check out before 11am

아침 식사는 식당에서 일곱시 반부터 아홉시까지입니다
ach'im shiksa-nŭn shiktang-esŏ ilkop-shi pan-put'ŏ ahop-shi-kkaji-imnida
breakfast is served in the restaurant between 7.30 and 9.00

아침에 신문 보시겠어요?
ach'im-e shimmun poshigessŏyo?
would you like a newspaper in the morning?

방이 아직 준비가 안 됐어요
pang-i ajik chumbi-ga an twaessŏyo
your room isn't ready yet

미니 바 사용하셨어요?
miniba sayonghashyŏssŏyo?
have you used the minibar?

가방은 여기 두셔도 돼요
kabang-ŭn yŏgi tushyŏdo twaeyo?
you can leave your bags here

YOUTH HOSTELS

Expressing yourself

do you have space for two people for tonight?
오늘 밤 두 사람 잘 방 있어요?
onŭl pam tu saram chal pang issŏyo?

we've booked two beds for three nights
침대 두 개 삼 일 동안 예약했는데요
ch'imdae tu gae sam il tongan yeyak'aennŭndeyo

ACCOMMODATION

45

could I leave my backpack at reception?
제 배낭 좀 카운터에 맡겨도 되나요?
che paenang chom k'aunt'ŏ-e makkyŏ-do twenayo?

do you have somewhere we could leave our bikes?
자전거 좀 놔 둘 데 있어요?
chajŏnggŏ chom nwa tul te issŏyo?

I'll come back for it around 7 o'clock
일곱 시쯤 다시 올게요
ilgop shi-tchŭm tashi olkkeyo

there's no hot water
뜨거운 물이 안 나와요
ttŭgŏun mul-i an nawayo

the sink's blocked
싱크가 막혔어요
singk'ŭ-ga mak'yŏssŏyo

Understanding

회원 카드 있으세요?
hwewon k'adŭ issŭseyo?
do you have a membership card?

침대 시트는 있어요
ch'imdae shit'ŭ-nŭn issŏyo
bed linen is provided

호스텔은 오후 여섯 시에 다시 엽니다
hosŭtel-ŭn ohu yŏsŏ shi-e tashi yŏmnida
the hostel reopens at 6pm

CAMPING

Expressing yourself

is there a campsite near here?
이 근처에 캠핑장 있어요?
i kŭnch'ŏ-e k'aemp'ingjang issŏyo?

I'd like to book a space for a two-person tent for three nights
삼 일동안 이인용 텐트 칠 장소를 예약하고 싶어요
sam il-dongan i-inyong t'ent'ŭ ch'il changso-rŭl yeyak'ago ship'ŏyo

how much is it a night?
하루에 얼마에요?
haru-e ŏlma-eyo?

where is the shower block?
샤워장은 어디에요?
shawojang-ŭn ŏdi-eyo?

can we pay, please? we were at space …
계산서 주세요. 장소는 … 이에요
kesansŏ chuseyo. changso-nŭn … -ieyo

Understanding

하루에 일인당 … 이에요
haru-e il-indang …-ieyo
it's … per person per night

뭐가 필요하시면 와서 말씀하세요
mŏ-ga p'ilyohashimy'ŏn wasŏ malssŭmhaseyo
if you need anything, just come and ask

EATING AND DRINKING

(i)

With its plentiful eating and drinking establishments, Korea is certainly never a place where you will need to go hungry … or thirsty! The most common kind of restaurant you will encounter are cheap 식당 *shiktang*, canteen-style establishments serving up mainly rice-based dishes. These are good places for a quick lunch or dinner, but do not serve alcohol. Prices start at around 3,000–5,000 won and service is fast – expect the food to be on your table within 5 minutes. A step above this, you will find Korean restaurants that specialize in, for example, meat-based dishes or raw fish and that usually serve alcohol as well.

In the large cities, restaurants serving Western food are becoming more popular. However, this is still mainly limited to fast food, pizza and pasta joints as well as hotel restaurants. Japanese-style restaurants are also widespread in the cities. Chinese food is generally limited to a Koreanized version based on a dish known as 자장면 *jajang-myŏn* (noodles in black bean sauce). The cities are also well stocked with bakeries and coffee shops.

In Korean restaurants, you will always be provided with water and side dishes as part of the service. In place of water, you may be given barley tea (보리차 *pori-ch'a*) instead. Note that the side dishes are bottomless – don't be afraid to ask for more! Attracting the waiter's attention with a shout of 여기요 *yŏgiyo* and showing him the empty dish usually does the trick, or you can ask 조금 더 주세요 *chogŭm tŏ chuseyo* ("could you give me a little more").

Koreans are known to like a drink or two and there are many different varieties of drinking establishment. Two of the most common varieties are the 소주집 *soju-chip*, which specializes in Korean *soju* (something like weak vodka) and the 호프집 *hop'ŭ-jip*, which serves draft beer. As Koreans like to have something to nibble on as they drink, most of these places will expect you to order side dishes. This does not apply to more Western-style bars.

At the majority of restaurants or drinking establishments, there is no need to ask for the bill. Simply pay at the exit as you leave. No service charge will be added and there is no need to leave a tip. Plusher Western restaurants may differ on some or all of these points.

Some cheap *shiktang* do not accept credit cards and a few ask for payment in advance (선불 *sŏnpul*), which is collected when you place your order.

When eating out, rather than splitting the bill, it is more common for one person to pay (often the person who did the inviting or who is the eldest). If you are treated to a meal, it is good manners to thank the person afterwards by saying 잘 먹었습니다 *chal mŏgŏssŭmnida* ("I ate well"). To say to your dining companions that you want to pay the bill, try 제가 낼게요 *che-ga naelkeyo* ("I'll pay"). If someone treats you to a meal, it is usually good manners to try to return the favour.

EATING AND DRINKING

The basics

beer	맥주 *maekchu*
bill	계산서 *kesansŏ*
black coffee	블랙커피 *pullek-k'ŏp'i*
bottle	병 *pyŏng*
bread	빵 *ppang*
breakfast	아침 *ach'im*
coffee	커피 *k'ŏp'i*
Coke®	콜라 *k'olla*
dessert	디저트 *tijŏt'u*, 후식 *hushik*
dinner	저녁 *chŏnyŏk*
fruit juice	과일 주스 *kwail chusŭ*
lemonade	레몬네이드 *remonneidŭ*, 사이다 *saida*
lunch	점심 *chŏmshim*
main course	메인코스 *mein-k'osŭ*
menu	메뉴 *menyui*, 차림표 *ch'arimp'yo*
mineral water	생수 *saengsu*
red wine	적포도주 *chŏkp'odoju*, 레드와인 *redŭ-wain*
rosé wine	로제와인 *roje-wain*
salad	샐러드 *saellŏdŭ*, 야채 *yachae*

sandwich	샌드위치 *saendŭwich'i*
service	서비스 *sŏbisŭ*
sparkling water	탄산수 *t'ansan-su*
sparkling wine	탄산포도주 *t'ansan-p'odoju*
starter	전식 *chŏnshik*, 스타터 *sŭt'at'ŏ*
still (water)	생수 *saengsu*
tea	차 *ch'a*
tip	봉사료 *pongsaryo*, 팁 *t'ip*
water	물 *mul*
white coffee	밀크커피 *milk'ŭ-k'ŏp'i*
white wine	백포도주 *paek-p'odoju*, 화이트와인 *hwait'u-wain*
wine	포도주 *p'odoju*, 와인 *wain*
wine list	와인 리스트 *wain lisŭt'ŭ*
to eat	먹어요 *mŏgŏyo*
to have breakfast	아침을 먹어요 *ach'im-ŭl mŏgŏyo*
to have dinner	저녁을 먹어요 *chŏnyŏk-ŭl mŏgŏyo*
to have lunch	점심을 먹어요 *chŏmsim-ŭl mŏgŏyo*
to order	주문해요 *chumunhaeyo*

Expressing yourself

shall we go and have something to eat?
어디 가서 뭐 좀 먹을까요?
ŏdi kasŏ mŏ chom mŏkŭlkkayo?

do you want to go for a drink?
뭐 좀 마시러 갈까요?
mŏ chom masirŏ kalkkayo?

can you recommend a good restaurant?
좋은 식당 좀 추천해 주세요
choŭn shiktang chom ch'uch'ŏnhae chuseyo

I'm not very hungry
배 안 고파요
pae an kop'ayo

excuse me! (to call the waiter)
여기요!
yŏgiyo!

cheers!
건배!
kŏmbae!

that was lovely
맛있어요
mash-issŏyo

could you bring us an ashtray, please?
재떨이 좀 주세요
chaettŏri chom chuseyo

where are the toilets, please?
화장실 어디 있어요?
hwajangshil ŏdi issŏyo?

Understanding

포장 *p'ojang*   takeaway
배달 *paedal*   delivery

죄송합니다. 11시에 마감입니다
chwesonghamnida. yŏlan-shi-e magam-imnida
I'm sorry, we stop serving at 11pm

RESERVING A TABLE

Expressing yourself

I'd like to reserve a table for tomorrow evening
내일 저녁 테이블 예약하고 싶은데요
naeil chŏnyŏk t'eibŭl yeyak'ago ship'ŭndeyo

for two people   **around 8 o'clock**
두 사람   여덟시 경
tu saram   *yŏdŏl-shi kyŏng*

do you have a table available any earlier than that?
그거보다 더 일찍 자리 없어요?
kŭgŏ-boda tŏ iltchik chari ŏpsŏyo?

I've reserved a table – the name's …
테이블 예약했는데요. 이름은 … 이에요
t'eibŭl yeyak'aennundeyo. irŭm-ŭn … i-eyo

Understanding

예약석 yeyaksŏk	reserved

몇 시에요?
myŏ shi-eyo?
for what time?

몇 분이에요?
myŏt pun-ieyo?
for how many people?

성함이 어떻게 되세요?
sŏngham-i ŏttŏk'e tweseyo?
what's the name?

담배 피우세요, 안 피우세요?
tambae p'iuseyo, an p'iuseyo?
smoking or non-smoking?

예약하셨어요?
yeyak'ashyŏssŏyo?
do you have a reservation?

이 구석 자리 괜찮으세요?
i kusŏk chari kwaench'anŭseyo?
is this table in the corner OK for you?

죄송하지만, 빈 자리가 없어요
chwesonghajiman, pin chari-ga ŏpsŏyo
I'm afraid we're full at the moment

ORDERING FOOD

Expressing yourself

yes, we're ready to order
네, 주문받으세요
ne, chumunbadŭseyo

no, could you give us a few more minutes?
아니오, 잠깐만 기다려 주세요
anio, chamkkanman kidaryŏ chuseyo

I'd like .../could I have ...?
… 주세요
... chuseyo

I'm not sure, what's "pibimbap"?
잘 모르겠는데 비빔밥이 뭐에요?
chal molŭgenunte pibimbap mŏ-eyo?

I'll have that
이거 주세요
igŏ chuseyo

does it come with vegetables?
이거 야채도 같이 나와요?
igŏ yach'ae-do kach'i nawayo?

what are today's specials?
오늘 특별 요리가 뭐에요?
onŭl t'ŭkpyŏl yori-ga mŏ-eyo?

what desserts do you have?
디저트 뭐 있어요?
tijŏt'ŭ mŏ issŏyo?

I'm allergic to nuts/wheat/seafood/citrus fruit
땅콩／밀／해산물／감귤 과일에 알레르기가 있어요
ttangk'ong/mil/haesanmul/kamgyul kwail-e allelŭgi-ga issŏyo

some water, please
물 좀 주세요
mul chom chuseyo

a bottle of red/white wine
적／백 포도주 한 병
chŏk/paek p'od'oju han pyŏng

that's for me
그거 저요
kŭgŏ chŏ-yo

this isn't what I ordered, I wanted …
제가 주문한 게 아니에요. … 주문했어요
che-ga chumunhan ke anieyo … chumunhaessŏyo

could you bring us some more water, please?
물 좀 더 주세요
mul chom tŏ chuseyo

Understanding

주문하시겠어요?
chumunhashigessŏyo?
are you ready to order?

잠시 후에 오겠습니다
chamshi hu-e ogessumnida
I'll come back in a few minutes

EATING AND DRINKING

🍴

뭐 드릴까요?	**죄송합니다. ⋯ 다 떨어졌어요**
mŏ tŭrilkkayo?	*chwesonghamnida … ta ttŏlŏjyŏssŏyo*
what would you like?	I'm sorry, we don't have any … left
맛있게 드세요	**음료수는 뭐 하시겠어요?**
mash-ikke tŭseyo	*ŭmryosu-nŭn mŏ hashigessŏyo?*
enjoy your meal	what would you like to drink?
디저트나 커피 하시겠어요?	**식사 맛있게 드셨어요?**
tijŏt'ŭ-na kŏp'i hashigessŏyo?	*shiksa mashikke tŭshyŏssŏyo?*
would you like dessert or coffee?	was everything OK?

BARS AND CAFÉS

Expressing yourself

I'd like …
⋯ 주세요
… chuseyo

a glass of white/red wine
백/적 포도주 한 잔
paek/chŏk p'od'oju han chan

a black/white coffee
블랙/밀크 커피
pŭllaek/milk'ŭ k'ŏp'i

a coffee and a piece of cake
커피하고 케익 한 조각
k'ŏp'i-hago k'eik han chogak

the same again, please
같은 거 한 잔 더 주세요
kat'ŭn kŏ han chan tŏ chuseyo

a Coke®/a diet Coke®
콜라/다이어트 콜라
k'olla/taiŏtŭ k'olla

a cup of tea
차 한 잔
ch'a han chan

a cup of hot chocolate
코코아 한 잔
k'ok'oa han chan

Understanding

무알콜 *mu-alk'ol*   non-alcoholic
알콜 없는 *alk'ol ŏmnun*   non-alcoholic

뭐 드시겠어요?
mŏ tŭshigessŏyo?
what would you like?

여기 금연석입니다
yŏgi kŭmyŏnsŏg-imnida
this is the non-smoking area

지금 계산해 주시겠어요?
chigum kesanhae chushigessŏyo?
could I ask you to pay now, please?

Some informal expressions

취했어요 *ch'wihaessŏyo* I'm drunk
필름이 끊겼어요 *p'illim-il kkŭngyŏssŏyo* I drank to the point of oblivion
(literally, I cut the film)
목까지 찼어요 *mok-kkaji ch'assŏyo* I'm stuffed
속이 더부룩해요 *sog-i tŏburukhaeyo* I've got indigestion
배고파서 죽겠어요 *pae-gop'asŏ chugessŏyo* I'm dying of hunger

THE BILL

Expressing yourself

the bill, please
계산서 주세요
kesansŏ chuseyo

how much do I owe you?
얼마에요?
ŏlma-eyo?

do you take credit cards?
신용카드 받아요?
shinyongk'adŭ padayo?

I think there's a mistake in the bill
계산이 잘못된 거 같은데요
kesan-i chalmottwen kŏ kat'ŭndeyo

is service included?
봉사료 포함돼 있어요?
pongsaryo p'ohamdwae issŏyo?

Understanding

전부 같이 계산하시겠어요?
chŏmbu kach'i kesanhashigessŏyo?
are you all paying together?

네, 봉사료 포함돼 있습니다
ney, pongsaryo p'ohamdwae issŭmnida
yes, service is included

FOOD AND DRINK

Most Korean meals feature three components: steamed rice (밥 *pap*), soups (국 *kuk*, 탕 *t'ang* or 찌개 *tchigae*) and side dishes (반찬 *panch'an*). Rice and/or soup may at times be replaced by noodles or noodle soup. Although your hotel may offer a Western-style breakfast and you may see hamburgers, spaghetti and pasta on the streets of South Korean cities, many Koreans will eat rice and soup three times a day.

Korean food is renowned for being eye-wateringly spicy and this especially applies to the peninsula's most prized culinary item: *kimch'i*. This fiery concoction basically consists of vegetables mixed with chilli, garlic, ginger and other ingredients, which have been left to ferment. 배추 김치 *paech'u kimch'i*. Chinese leaf *kimch'i* is the most popular variety, but it can also be made from radishes, spring onions, cucumbers and many other vegetables. Not only does *kimch'i* make its way onto practically every Korean dining table as a side dish, but it can also be used as the principal ingredient in dishes such as 김치찌개 *kimch'i-tchigae* (*kimch'i* stew) or 김치볶음밥 *kimch'i-pokkŭm-pap* (*kimch'i* fried rice).

Many soups are meat- or seafood-based, with anchovies (멸치 *myo˘lch'i*) being a common ingredient. Although it may at times be difficult to find vegetarian or vegan main dishes, many side dishes contain only seasoned vegetables.

♦ Soups and stews

Korea has three main types of soups or stew. 국 *kuk* and 탕 *t'ang* are thinner, more watery soups, with the latter being more meat- or seafood-based. 찌개 *tchigae* are more like thick stews made with larger amounts of vegetables. All of these soups are served with steamed rice.

콩나물국 *k'ongnamul-kuk*　　　　　beansprout soup; a light soup, usually
　　　　　　　　　　　　　　　　　vegetarian

만두국 *mandu-kuk*	dumpling soup; made with stuffed dumplings (usually stuffed with meat) similar to dim sum
미역국 *miyŏk-kuk*	seaweed soup; eaten by all Koreans on their birthdays, often made with meat
떡국 *ttŏk-kuk*	rice-cake soup; made by boiling savoury rice cakes in broth
갈비탕 *kalbi-t'ang*	rib soup; wholesome meaty soup containing big chunky beef ribs
설렁탕 *sŏllŏng-t'ang*	milky broth made from beef bones and heaped with strips of beef and thin noodles
매운탕 *maeun-t'ang*	spicy soup; fish stew made with suicidal quantities of chilli!
해물탕 *haemul-t'ang*	seafood soup; spicy soup containing lots of fish, squid and shellfish
삼계탕 *samge-t'ang*	soup containing a whole (small) chicken stuffed with ginseng and rice – guaranteed to boost your energy
김치찌개 *kimch'i-tchigae*	*kimch'i* stew; commonly prepared using strips of pork
된장찌개 *twenjang-tchigae*	soybean-paste soup; Korea's version of miso soup, only thicker and more wholesome
순두부찌개 *sun-tubu- tchigae*	soft tofu stew; tofu, egg and clams in a spicy soup

♦ Rice dishes

볶음밥 *pokkŭm-pap* are fried rice dishes, whereas 덮밥 *tŏp-pap* are dishes that are served on a bed of boiled rice.

| 김치볶음밥 *kimch'i-pokkŭm-pap* | *kimch'i* fried rice; rice fried in fiery hot *paechu kimch'i* |
| 오징어덮밥 *ojingŏ-tŏp-pap* | squid on rice; squid with vegetables in a tangy hot sauce |

FOOD AND DRINK

제육덮밥 *jeyuk-tŏp-pap*	pork on rice; strips of pork fried with vegetables and heaps of chilli paste
오므라이스 *omŭraisŭ*	fried rice wrapped in an omelette (the name comes from omelette + rice)
비빔밥 *pibimbap*	rice with lots of fresh vegetables topped with egg and chilli paste – mix together at the table for a quick and healthy Korean speciality

♦ Noodle dishes

Commonly served without rice, a bowl of noodles is usually a filling enough meal by itself. However, 냉면 *naengmyŏn* are also sometimes eaten after meat dishes (see below).

라면 *ramyŏn*	like Japanese ramen, but almost always made from instant noodles and with a spicy kick
칼국수 *k'alguksu*	thick-cut noodles in seafood-flavoured broth
냉면 *naengmyŏn*	cold buckwheat noodles served either in an icy broth (물냉면 *mulnaengmyŏn*) or with a spicy sauce (비빔냉면 *pibimnaengmyŏn*) for a totally unique taste
콩국수 *k'ongguksu*	more cold noodles, this time in a thick soup packed with beans
잡채 *chapch'ae*	noodles mixed with meat and vegetables
자장면 *chajangmyŏn*	noodles in a thick black bean sauce, said to be of Chinese origin

FOOD AND DRINK

♦ Meat dishes

Although most Korean dishes are light on meat, when Koreans do go carnivore they do it in a big way. All the dishes below are grilled on a hotplate at the table. Although staff may lend a hand, basically you are doing your own cooking. The meat is typically eaten dipped in a sauce made of soybean paste and then wrapped in a lettuce or sesame leaf. Eating this way is a leisurely social affair and is generally accompanied by more than a glass or two of 소주 *soju* (see p. 65). If you are still hungry after all that meat, you can fill up on 된장찌개 *twenjang-tchigae* (soybean-paste soup) and rice or 냉면 *naengmyo˜n* (cold buckwheat noodles).

갈비 *kalbi*	beef ribs grilled at the table
돼지갈비 *twaeji-kalbi*	pork ribs grilled at the table
삼겹살 *samgyŏpsal*	belly pork grilled at the table
불고기 *pulgogi*	marinated beef grilled at the table
닭갈비 *tak-kalbi*	spicy chicken and vegetables fried in a big pan in front of you – leave a little at the end, order rice and you can finish your meal off with chicken fried rice!
보쌈 *possam*	slices of succulent boiled pork served with cabbage and a particularly pungent *kimch'i*

♦ Seafood dishes

Just about anything that lives in the sea makes its way onto the Korean dining table. For the full seafood experience, make it to the east coast and eat your seafood right on the seashore – you'll never taste anything fresher.

회 *hwe*	raw fish, equivalent to Japanese sashimi but eaten dipped in chilli sauce as well as soy sauce

FOOD AND DRINK

초밥 *ch'obap*   equivalent to sushi
게장 *kejang*   crab marinated in either a soy sauce
                                       or a chilli-based sauce
생선구이 *saengsŏn-gui*   grilled fish
낙지볶음 *nakji-pokkŭm*   fried octopus
장어구이 *changŏ-gui*   grilled eel

♦ Snacking Korean-style

Looking for a quick bite to eat but fancy something more adventurous than a burger? Then simply pop into a 포장마차 *p'ojangmach'a* (streetside stall) or 분식점 *punshikchŏm* (snack bar) for a bite to eat Korean-style.

김밥 *kimbap*   rice rolled in seaweed and commonly
                                       stuffed with spinach, radish, carrot,
                                       ham, etc
떡볶이 *ttŏkpokki*   savoury rice cakes cooked swimming
                                       in potent chilli sauce – *the* ubiquitous
                                       street food of South Korea
순대 *sundae*   pig's blood sausage stuffed with glass
                                       noodles – a distant cousin of British
                                       black pudding
튀김 *t'wigim*   equivalent to Japanese tempura –
                                       deep-fried vegetables and seafood
만두 *mandu*   dumplings stuffed with meat and tofu,
                                       similar to dim sum
오뎅 *odeng*   pressed fishcake

♦ Korean sweets

Still hungry after all that rice, noodles, meat and seafood? Then how about something a little bit sweeter? Note however that traditional Korean sweets don't pack anything of the sugar kick of Western cakes and candies – the taste generally borders on the savoury.

호떡 *hottŏk*   cinnamon pancake with sugary filling

붕어빵 *pungŏppang*	fish-shaped cake with red bean filling – look out for the fish-shaped moulds they are baked in
떡 *ttŏk*	cakes made with rice flour and with a range of different fillings and toppings
팥빙수 *papp'ingsu*	shaved ice topped with red bean paste and other goodies
엿 *yŏt*	traditional sticky toffee

♦ Side dishes

Side dishes can come in all shapes and sizes, so it would be impossible to list them all here. The first four are usually ordered on their own. The latter are examples of the kind of side dishes that are thrown in for free at all good Korean restaurants

전 *chŏn*	pan-fried battered vegetables, meat or seafood
빈대떡 *pindaettŏk*	savoury pancakes prepared with large quantities of vegetables or seafood; sometimes (misleadingly) referred to as "Korean pizza"
두부김치 *tubu-kimch'i*	tofu accompanied with fried *kimch'i*
골뱅이 *kolbaengi*	spicy bai top shells (a type of whelk) with mixed vegetables
김치 *kimch'i*	Korea's national dish (see above)!
깍두기 *kkaktugi*	cubes of radish *kimch'i*
오이소박이 *oi-sobagi*	stuffed cucumber
나물 *namul*	generic term for various leaves and greens, generally served lightly cooked and flavoured
김 *kim*	dried seaweed sheets made for rolling with rice

♦ Something for the more adventurous

Korea's more unusual culinary tastes even make headline news in the West or are more frequently quoted for cheap laughs by desperate comedians. Most of these foods are eaten primarily by older Koreans, especially males.

보신탕 *poshin-t'ang*	dog-meat soup and Korea's most controversial food; traditionally eaten as an energy-booster in the sapping midsummer heat
산낙지 *sannakchi*	live octopus cut into pieces and eaten while still wriggling
번데기 *pŏndegi*	silkworm larvae sold by street vendors from steaming pots
해삼 *haesam*	sea cucumber, best eaten raw

♦ Condiments

소금 *sogum*	salt
후추 *huch'u*	pepper
케첩 *k'ech'ŏp*	ketchup
마요네즈 *mayonejŭ*	mayonnaise
겨자 *kyŏja*	mustard
간장 *kanjang*	soy sauce
참기름 *chamgirŭm*	sesame oil
와사비 *wasabi*	wasabi
고추장 *kochu'jang*	chilli sauce
쌈장 *ssamjang*	sauce made from soybean paste, usually eaten with meat
식초 *shikch'o*	vinegar
핫소스 *hasosŭ*	"hot sauce": Tabasco sauce – used by Koreans to spice up pizza
피클 *p'ik'ul*	pickles – another pizza accompaniment
치즈가루 *ch'ijŭ-karu*	powdered Parmesan cheese for pizzas and pastas

FOOD AND DRINK

◆ Fruit and vegetables

The vast majority of fruit and vegetables eaten in South Korea are grown locally. As a consequence, you may find that the time of year and climatic conditions have a larger influence on the kind of produce available and the market price than they do at home.

Koreans go for fruit in a big way. If you are invited to a Korean home, expect fruit to appear either as a snack or as dessert. It will generally be served sliced on a communal plate and eaten using tiny fruit forks. Fruit also makes a good gift to give your hosts. At 추석 *ch'usok* (harvest festival) and 설날 *sŏlnal* (lunar new year), look out for the huge gift boxes of fruit being sold by the truckload.

가지 *kaji*	aubergine
감자 *kamja*	potato
고추 *koch'u*	chilli pepper
깻잎 *kkaenip*	sesame leaf
고구마 *koguma*	sweet potato
당근 *tanggŭn*	carrot
무 *mu*	radish
배추 *paech'u*	Chinese leaf
부추 *puch'u*	spring onion
상추 *sangch'u*	lettuce
시금치 *shigŭmch'i*	spinach
양배추 *yang-paechu*	cabbage
양파 *yang-p'a*	onion
오이 *oi*	cucumber
참외 *ch'amwe*	a type of small melon with edible seeds
토마토 *t'omat'o*	tomato
파 *p'a*	spring onion
피망 *p'imang*	pepper
호박 *hobak*	courgette; pumpkin
귤 *kyul*	mandarin orange
딸기 *ttalgi*	strawberry
멜론 *mellon*	melon

FOOD AND DRINK

바나나 *panana*	banana
배 *pae*	pear
복 복숭아 *poksunga*	peach
사과 *sagwa*	apple
살구 *salgu*	apricot
수박 *subak*	watermelon
앵두 *aengdu*	cherry
오렌지 *orenji*	orange
자두 *chadu*	plum
키위 *k'iwi*	kiwi
파인애플 *p'ainaep'ŭl*	pineapple
포도 *p'odo*	grapes

♦ Alcoholic drinks

South Korea is packed with bars of all description and the vast majority of meat and seafood restaurants also serve alcohol.

Although Koreans are big beer drinkers, some may find the range of beers available to be somewhat disappointing, with three large local brands – Cass, Hite and OB – dominating the market. Although bottled Japanese, European and American beers are also available, the difference in price can be quite steep.

Beer, however, cannot compete for popularity with Korea's national obsession: 소주 *soju*. Rather like weak vodka, *soju* has a clear and fresh taste and goes well with Korean meat and seafood dishes. *Soju* can also be flavoured, most typically with lemon, or can appear in cocktails. Other local alcohols listed below also come highly recommended.

양주 *yangju*	"Western alcohol"; used to refer to Western spirits, typically whisky
포도주 *p'odoju*	wine
맥주 *maekchu*	beer
소주 *soju*	*soju* – Korea's number-one tipple (see above)
막걸리 *makkŏlli*	unfiltered rice wine; a delicious and refreshing milky white wine – just

watch out for the headaches the
next morning!

동동주 tongdongju — essentially an upmarket version of
makkŏlli – filtered, clear rice wine

매실주 maeshilju — sweet plum wine

정종 chŏngjong — equivalent to Japanese sake

♦ Tea

Although Koreans may not go in for tea as much as their Chinese or Japanese neighbours, there are still quite a few local brews worth tasting.

보리차 porich'a — barley tea, often drunk or provided
free at restaurants in place of
water – hot in winter and chilled in
summer

옥수수차 oksusuch'a — corn tea, also served like *porich'a*

녹차 nokch'a — green tea

둥굴레차 tunggullech'a — a refreshing everyday tea made
from the leaves of a plant called
Solomon's seal

유자차 yujach'a — citrus tea

모과차 mogwach'a — quince tea

율무차 yulmuch'a — thick wholesome tea made from adlay
(the seeds of a wild grass)

GOING OUT

Seoul and the other large cities in South Korea offer excellent opportunities for nightlife and other entertainment. After a few drinks at the *sojubang* or *hop'u-jip* (see the Eating and Drinking chapter), what better way to let off steam than going to the 노래방 *noraebang* (karaoke parlour)? Nightclubs (나이트 *nait'ŭ* or 클럽 *k'ŭllŏp*) are also widespread.

Gambling is highly restricted in Korea. You will find casinos at a few of the luxury hotels, but entry is limited to non-Korean nationals.

Cinemas are plentiful and reasonably priced. Foreign films are shown in the original language with Korean subtitles. Korea's own movie industry has boomed in recent years; however, local showings of these films with English subtitles are rare.

Seoul also has a good theatre scene. As well as imported forms of performance art, Korean traditional music and dance also come highly recommended. 판소리 *pansori* – an epic narrative performed through song and percussion – is one Korean speciality.

For cinema and theatre listings, check out the Friday editions of the English language newspapers *The Korea Times* and *The Korea Herald*.

The basics

ballet	발레 *palle*
band	밴드 *paendŭ*
bar	바 *pa*, 빠 *ppa*
cinema	영화관 *yŏnghwagwan*, 극장 *kŭkjang*
circus	서커스 *sŏk'ŏsŭ*
classical music	고전음악 *kojŏnŭmak*
club	클럽 *k'ŭllŏp*, 나이트 *nait'ŭ*
concert	음악회 *ŭmak'we*
festival	축제 *ch'ukche*
film	영화 *yŏnghwa*
folk music	민속음악 *minsokŭmak*

group	그룹 *kŭrup*
jazz	재즈 *chaejŭ*
modern dance	현대무용 *hyŏndaemuyong*
musical	뮤지컬 *myujik'ŏl*
opera	오페라 *op'era*
party	파티 *p'at'i*
play	연극 *yŏnggŭk*
pop music	팝 음악 *p'ap ŭmak*
rock music	록 음악 *rok ŭmak*
show	쑈 *sshyo*
subtitled film	자막 영화 *chamak yŏnghwa*
theatre	극장 *kŭkchang*
ticket	표 *pyo*
to book	예약해요 *yeyak'aeyo*
to go out	나가요 *nagayo*

SUGGESTIONS AND INVITATIONS

Expressing yourself

where can we go?
어디 갈까요?
ŏdi kalkkayo?

what do you want to do?
뭐 하고 싶어요?
mŏ hago ship'ŏyo?

shall we go for a drink?
한잔 하러 갈까요?
han-jan harŏ kalkkayo?

what are you doing tonight?
오늘 밤에 뭐 해요?
onŭl pam-e mŏ haeyo?

do you have plans?
무슨 약속 있어요?
musŭn yaksok issŏyo?

would you like to …?
… 하고 싶어요?
… hago shipŏyo?

we were thinking of going to …
… 에 갈까 생각해요
…-e kalkka saenggak'aeyo

I can't today, but maybe some other time
오늘은 안 돼요. 다음에 하지요
onŭl-ŭn an twaeyo. taŭm-e hajiyo

I'm not sure I can make it
갈 수 있을지 없을지 잘 모르겠어요
kal su issŭlji ŏpsŭlji chal morŭgessŏyo

I'd love to
네, 너무 좋아요
ne, nŏmu choayo

ARRANGING TO MEET

Expressing yourself

what time shall we meet?
몇 시에 만날까요?
myŏt si-e mannalkkayo?

where shall we meet?
어디서 만날까요?
ŏdisŏ mannalkkayo?

would it be possible to meet a bit later?
좀 늦게 만날 수 있을까요?
chom nŭkke mannal su issŭlkkayo?

I have to meet ... at nine
... 아홉시에 만나야 돼요
... ahop-si-e mannaya twaeyo

I don't know where it is but I'll find it on the map
어디인지 잘 모르지만 지도에서 찾아보겠어요
ŏdi-inji chal morŭjiman chido-esŏ ch'aja-bogessŏyo

see you tomorrow night
내일 밤에 만나요
naeil pam-e mannayo

I'll meet you later, I have to stop by the hotel first
잠시 후에 만나요. 먼저 호텔에 좀 들러야 돼요
chamshi hu-e mannayo. mŏnjŏ hot'el-e chom tŭllŏya twaeyo

I'll call/text you if there's a change of plan
약속 변경되면 전화/문자 할게요
yaksok pyŏnggyŏngtwemyŏn chŏnhwa/munja halkeyo

GOING OUT

69

are you going to eat beforehand?
먼저 식사하시겠어요?
mǒnjǒ shiksahashigessǒyo?

sorry I'm late
늦어서 미안합니다
nǔjǒsǒ mianhamnida

Understanding

이거 괜찮아요?
igǒ kwaench'anayo?
is that OK with you?

거기서 만나요
kǒgi-sǒ mannayo
I'll meet you there

여덟시 경에 모시러 올게요
yǒdǒl-shi moshirǒ olgeyo
I'll come and pick you up about 8

밖에서 만나요
pakkesǒ mannayo
we can meet outside

내 전화번호를 드릴게요. 내일 전화하세요
ne chǒnhwa-bǒnho-rǔl tǔrilkeyo. naeil chǒnhwahaseyo
I'll give you my number and you can call me tomorrow

Some informal expressions

맥주나 한잔 합시다 *maekchu-na han-jan hapshida* let's go for a beer
이차 갑시다 *i-ch'a kapshida* let's go to the second place (meaning
"let's go and drink/party somewhere else". Koreans like to move
around when on a night out and list the different places they go as *il/i/
sam/sa/o* "the first/second/third/fourth/fifth".)
십팔번이 뭐에요? *ship-p'al-bǒn-i mǒ-eyo?* what's your number 18?
(meaning "what song can you sing best?", used in the karaoke parlour)

FILMS, SHOWS AND CONCERTS

Expressing yourself

is there a guide to what films/performances are on?
영화／공연 안내서 있어요?
yŏnghwa/kongyŏn annaesŏ issŏyo?

I'd like two tickets for …
… 표 두 장 주세요
… pyo tu chang chuseyo

two tickets, please
두 장 주세요
tu chang chuseyo

it's called …
이름이 …이에요
irum-i …-ieyo

I've seen the trailer
예고편을 봤어요
yegop'yŏn-ŭl passŏyo

what time does it start?
몇 시에 시작해요?
myŏt shi-e shijak'aeyo?

I'd like to go and see a show
공연을 보러 가고 싶어요
kongyŏn-ŭl porŏ kago ship'ŏyo

I'll find out whether there are still tickets available
아직 표가 있는지 알아 볼게요
ajik p'yo-ga innŭnji ara polgeyo

do we need to book in advance?
미리 예약해야 돼요?
miri yeyak'aeya twaeyo?

how long is it on for?
얼마동안 해요?
ŏlmadongan haeyo?

are there tickets for another day?
다른 날 표도 있어요?
tarŭn nal p'yo-do issŏyo?

I'd like to go and do karaoke
노래방에 가고 싶어요
noraebang-e kago ship'ŏyo

are there any free concerts?
무료 음악회 있어요?
muryo ŭmak'we issŏyo?

GOING OUT

what sort of music is it?
무슨 음악이에요?
musŭn ŭmak-ieyo?

Understanding

예약 *yeyak* — bookings

매표소 *maep'yoso* — box office

취소 *chwiso* — cancelled

…부터 일반 공개 *put'ŏ ilban konggae* — on general release from …

마티네 *mat'ine* — matinée

오후 공연 *ohu kongyŏn* — matinée

야외 음악회예요
yawe ŭmak'we-eyo
it's an open-air concert

좋은 평을 받았어요
choŭn p'yŏng-ŭl padassŏyo
it's had very good reviews

다음 주에 공개돼요
taŭm chu-e konggaedwaeyo
it comes out next week

CGV에서 여덟시부터예요
CGV-esŏ yŏdŏl-shi-put'ŏ-eyo
it's on at 8pm at CGV

그 공연은 매진이에요
ku kongyŏn-ŭn maejin-ieyo
that showing's sold out

… 까지 전부 매진이에요
… kkaji chŏmbu maejin-ieyo
it's all booked up until …

미리 예약할 필요 없어요
miri yeyak'al p'iryo ŏpsŏyo
there's no need to book in advance

연극은 휴식 시간 포함해서 한 시간 반이에요
yŏnggŭk-ŭn hyushik shigan p'ohamhaesŏ han shigan pan-ieyo
the play lasts an hour and a half, including the interval

프로그램 사시겠어요?
p'ŭrogŭraem sashigessŏyo?
would you like to buy a programme?

휴대 전화를 꺼 주세요
hyudae chŏnhwa-rul kkŏ chuseyo
please turn off your mobile phones

GOING OUT

PARTIES AND CLUBS

Expressing yourself

I'm having a little leaving party tonight
오늘 밤 환송파티 해요
onŭl pam hwansongp'ati haeyo

should I bring something to drink?
마실 거 가지고 갈까요?
mashil kŏ kajigo kalkkayo?

we could go to a club afterwards
그 후에 클럽에 갈지도 몰라요
ku hu-e k'ŭllŏp-e kaljido mollayo

do you have to pay to get in?
입장료 있어요?
ipchangnyo issŏyo?

I have to meet someone inside
안에 있는 사람을 만나야 돼요
an-e innŭn saram-ŭl mannaya twaeyo

will you let me back in when I come back?
돌아올 때 입장시켜 주세요
toraol ttae ipchangshik'yŏ chuseyo

the DJ's really cool
저 디제이 정말 멋있어요
chŏ tijei chŏngmal mŏshissŏyo

do you come here often?
여기 자주 오세요?
yŏgi chaju oseyo?

can I buy you a drink?
한 잔 하시겠어요?
han chan hashigessŏyo?

thanks, but I'm with my boyfriend
아니요. 남자친구하고 같이 왔어요
aniyo, namjach'ingu-hago kach'i wassŏyo

no thanks, I don't smoke
아니요, 담배 안 피워요
aniyo, tambae an p'iwŏyo

Understanding

음료수 무료 *umnyosu muryo*	free drink
휴대폼 보관소 *hyudaep'um pogwanso*	cloakroom
자정 이후 오만원 *chajŏng ihu omanwon*	5,000 won after midnight

수진 집에서 파티가 있어요
Su-jin chip-esŏ p'ati-ka issŏyo
there's a party at Su-jin's place

한 잔 하시겠어요?
han jan hashigessŏyo?
can I buy you a drink?

담배 있어요?
tambae issŏyo?
have you got a cigarette?

집까지 모셔다 드릴까요?
chip-kkaji moshyŏda tŭrilkkayo?
can I see you home?

춤 추시겠어요?
ch'um ch'ushigessŏyo?
do you want to dance?

라이터 있어요?
raitŏ issŏyo?
have you got a light?

또 만날 수 있을까요?
tto mannal su issŭlkkayo?
can we see each other again?

GOING OUT

TOURISM AND SIGHTSEEING

In South Korea, KTO (Korea Tourism Organization) represents the most reliable source of tourist information. As well as offices at Incheon International Airport and downtown Seoul, the company operates a 24-hour travel information and assistance phone line with Korean-English bilingual operators – just dial 1330. KTO also has several overseas branches, including centres in London, Sydney and New York and a useful website (english.tour2korea.com).

For visits to North Korea, your principal sources of information will be your tour organizer and your local North Korean guides. Koryo Tours (www.koryogroup.com) is a Beijing-based company that specializes in organizing travel to North Korea. Their website also provides a good starting point if you are thinking about a trip to the North.

The basics

ancient	고대 *kodae*
antique	골동품 *koldongp'um*
area	지역 *chiyŏk*
castle	성 *sŏng*
century	세기 *segi*
church	교회 *kyohwe*; *(Catholic)* 성당 *sŏngdang*
exhibition	전시회 *chŏnshihwe*
gallery	미술관 *misulgwan*
modern art	현대 미술 *hyŏndae misul*
museum	박물관 *pangmulgwan*
painting	회화 *hwehwa*
park	공원 *kongwon*
ruins	폐허 *p'ehŏ*
sculpture	조각 *chogak*
statue	동상 *tongsang*

street map	지도 *chido*
temple	절 *chŏl*
tour guide	관광 가이드 *kwanggwang kaidŭ*
tourist	관광객 *kwanggwanggaek*
tourist office	관광 안내소 *kwanggwang annaeso*
town centre	시내 *shinae*

Expressing yourself

I'd like some information on …
… 에 대한 정보를 알고 싶어요
…-e taehan chŏngbo-rŭl algo ship'ŏyo

can you tell me where the tourist office is?
관광 안내소가 어디 있어요?
kwanggwang annaeso-ga ŏdi issŏyo?

do you have a street map of the town?
이 마을 지도 있어요?
i maŭl chido issŏyo?

I was told there's an old temple you can visit
오래된 절이 있다고 들었어요
oraedwen chŏl-i ittago tŭrŏssŏyo

can you show me where it is on the map?
지도에서 가르쳐 주세요
chido-esŏ karŭch'yŏ chuseyo

how do you get there?
거기 어떻게 가요?
kŏgi ŏttŏk'e kayo?

is it free?
무료에요?
muryo-eyo?

when was it built?
언제 세워졌어요?
ŏnje sewojyŏssŏyo?

where is the ticket office?
매표소가 어디에요?
maep'yoso-ga ŏdi-eyo?

does the guide speak English?
가이드가 영어 해요?
kaidŭ-ga yŏngŏ haeyo?

Understanding

입장무료 *ipchangmuryo*	admission free
폐관 *p'egwan*	closed
전쟁 *chŏnjaeng*	war
침략 *ch'imnyak*	invasion
중세 *chungse*	medieval
개관 *kaegwan*	open
조선 *chosŏn*	Choson
중국 *chungguk*	China
일본 *ilbon*	Japan
개장 *kaejang*	renovation
보수공사 *posugongsa*	restoration work
고도 *kodo*	old town
가이드 관광 *kaidŭ kwanggwang*	guided tour
현재 위치 *hyŏnjae wich'i*	you are here *(on a map)*

도착해서 물어 봐 주세요
toch'ak'aesŏ mulŏ pa chuseyo
you'll have to ask when you get there

이 다음 가이드 투어는 두 시에 시작합니다
i taŭm kaidŭ t'uŏ-nŭn tu shi-e shijak'amnida
the next guided tour starts at 2 o'clock

MUSEUMS, EXHIBITIONS AND MONUMENTS

Expressing yourself

I've heard there's a very good ... exhibition on at the moment
현재 아주 좋은 … 전시회가 있다고 들었는데요
hyŏnjae aju cho-ŭn … chŏnshihwe-ga ittago tŭrŏnnŭndeyo

how much is it to get in?
입장료가 얼마에요?
ipchangnyo-ga ŏlma-eyo?

is this ticket valid for the exhibition as well?
이 표로 전시회도 들어갈 수 있어요?
i p'yo-ro chŏnshihwe-do tŭrŏgal su issŏyo?

are there any discounts for young people?
학생 할인 있어요?
haksaeng halin issŏyo?

is it open on Sundays?
일요일에도 해요?
ilyoil-e-do haeyo?

two adults and one child, please
어른 두 명하고 어린이 한 명요
ŏrŭn tu myŏng-hago ŏrin-i han myŏng-yo

I have a student card
학생증이 있어요
haksaengjŭng-i issŏyo

Understanding

오디오 가이드 *odio kaidŭ*	audioguide
매표소 *maep'yoso*	ticket office
임시 전시회 *imshi chŏnshihwe*	temporary exhibition
상설 전시회 *sangsŏl chŏnshihwe*	permanent exhibition
플래시 금지 *p'ŭllaeshi kŭmji*	no flash photography
사진 촬영 금지 *sajin ch'walyŏng kŭmji*	no photography
이쪽으로 가십시오 *i-tchok-ŭro kashipshio*	this way
정숙 *chŏngsuk*	silence, please
손 대지 마세요 *son taeji maseyo*	please do not touch

박물관 입장료는 … 입니다
pangmulgwan ipchangnyo-nŭn … -imnida
admission to the museum costs …

TOURISM, SIGHTSEEING

이 표로 전시회도 입장할 수 있습니다
i p'yo-ro chŏnshihwe-do ipchanghal su issŭmnida
this ticket also allows you access to the exhibition

학생증 있으세요?
haksaengjŭng issŭseyo?
do you have your student card?

GIVING YOUR IMPRESSIONS

Expressing yourself

it's beautiful
멋있어요
mŏshissŏyo

it's fantastic
훌륭해요
hullyunghaeyo

I really enjoyed it
정말 재미있었어요
chŏngmal chaemi-issŏssŏyo

it was a bit boring
좀 지루했어요
chom chiruhaessŏyo

I'm not really a fan of modern art
현대 미술엔 흥미가 좀 없어요
hyŏndae misul-en hŭngmi-ga chom ŏpsŏyo

it's expensive for what it is
내용에 비해 좀 비싸요
naeyong-e pihae chom pissayo

it's very touristy
좀 관광지 냄새가 나요
chom kwanggwangji naemsae-ga nayo

it was really crowded
아주 복잡했어요
aju pokchap'aessŏyo

it was beautiful
멋있었어요
mŏshissŏssŏyo

it was fantastic
훌륭했어요
hullyunghaessŏyo

I didn't like it that much
그저 그랬어요
kujŏ kŭraessŏyo

we didn't go in the end, the queue was too long
줄이 너무 길어서 결국 안 들어갔어요
chul-i nŏmu kilŏsŏ kyŏlguk an tŭlŏgassŏyo

we didn't have time to see everything
시간이 없어서 다 못 봤어요
shigan-i ŏpsŏsŏ ta mot passŏyo

Understanding

유명한 *yumyŏnghan*	famous
그림 같은 *kŭrim kat'ŭn*	picturesque
전형적인 *chŏnhyŏngjŏgin*	typical
전통적인 *chŏnt'ongjŏgin*	traditional

… 꼭 가서 보세요
… kkok kasŏ poseyo
you really must go and see …

… 가시라고 추천하고 싶어요
… kashirago ch'uch'ŏnhago ship'ŏyo
I recommend going to …

도시 전체를 한눈에 잘 볼 수 있어요
toshi chŏnch'e-rŭl hannun-e chal pol su issŏyo
there's a wonderful view over the whole city

좀 관광지 냄새가 나요
chom kwanggwangji naemsae-ga nayo
it's become a bit too touristy

해변이 완전히 폐허가 됐어요
haebyŏn-i wanjŏnhi p'ehŏ-ga twaessŏyo
the coast has been completely ruined

SPORTS AND GAMES

The most popular spectator sports in South Korea are baseball, followed by basketball and football. International football games are passionately supported and well worth attending for the atmosphere – who could forget the Korean fans at the 2002 World Cup? However, unfortunately the local K-league suffers from low attendances.

Korea has good facilities for golf, with plentiful courses and driving ranges. The cold winters and mountains also make Korea a good choice for skiing, with several resorts located within a short drive of Seoul. The mountains are also popular destinations for hiking – on sunny weekends in spring or autumn, expect popular hiking destinations to be extremely busy.

Native Korean sports include *taekwondo* (태권도) and several other martial arts. 씨름 *sshirum*, a type of wrestling, is also popular. As for games, Koreans enjoy 고스톱 *go-stop* (a game played with small cards with flower designs, originally from Japan), 바둑 *paduk* (rather like draughts) and 장기 *changgi* (similar to chess). More traditional activities include 윷놀이 *yut-nori* (a board game played by throwing small sticks instead of dice), 널뛰기 *nŏl-ttwigi* (a type of rustic see-saw) and 재기 차기 *chaegi ch'agi* (a game using a bean-filled cloth ball, similar to the American game hacky sack).

The basics

ball	공 *kong*
baseball	야구 *yagu*
basketball	농구 *nongu*
cards	카드 *k'adŭ*
chess	체스 *ch'esŭ*, 장기 *changgi*
cross-country skiing	크로스컨츄리 스키 *kŭrosŭk'ŏnch'yuri sŭk'i*
cycling	사이클 *saik'ŭl*
downhill skiing	활강 스키 *hwalgang sŭk'i*
football	축구 *ch'ukku*

golf	골프 kolp'ŭ
hiking path	등산 코스 tŭngsan k'osŭ
match	경기 kyŏnggi
mountain biking	마운틴 바이크 maunt'in paik'ŭ
pool (game)	포켓볼 p'ok'et-pol; (Korean version) 당구 tanggu
rugby	럭비 rŏgbi
ski	스키 sŭk'i
snowboarding	스노우 보드 sŭnou podŭ
sport	스포츠 spo'ch'ŭ, 운동 undong
surfing	서핑 sŏp'ing
swimming	수영 suyŏng
swimming pool	수영장 suyŏngjang
table tennis	탁구 t'akku
tennis	테니스 t'enisŭ
trip	여행 yŏhaeng
wrestling	씨름 sshirum
to go for a walk	산책 해요 sanch'aek'aeyo
to go hiking	등산해요 tŭngsanhaeyo
to have a game of ...	… 게임 해요 … keim haeyo
to play	… 해요 … haeyo

Expressing yourself

I'd like to hire ... for an hour
… 한 시간동안 빌리고 싶어요
… han shigan-dongan pilligo sh'ip'oyo

can I book for an hour?
한 시간동안 예약해 주세요?
han shigan-dongan yeyak'ae chuseyo?

are there ... lessons available?
… 레슨 받을 수 있어요?
… resŭn padŭl su issŏyo?

do you have a timetable?
시간표 있어요?
shigan-p'yo issŏyo?

how much is it per person per hour?
한 사람당 한 시간에 얼마에요?
han saram-dang han shigan-e ŏlma-eyo?

I'm not very sporty
운동신경이 별로 안 좋아요
undong-shingyŏng-i pyŏllo an choayo

I've never done it before
한번도 해 본적이 없어요
han-bŏn-do hae ponjŏk-i ŏpsŏyo

I've done it once or twice, a long time ago
아주 오래 전에 한 두 번 해 봤어요
aju orae chŏn-e han tu pŏn hae passŏyo

I'm exhausted!
완전히 지쳤어요
wanjŏnhi chich'yŏssŏyo

I'd like to go and watch a football match
가서 축구 경기 보고 싶어요
kasŏ ch'ukku kyŏnggi pogo shipŏyo

Understanding

렌트 *rentŭ*		for hire
대여 *taeyŏ*		for hire

경험이 있으세요? 아니면 완전 초보이세요?
kyŏnghŏm-i issŭseyo? animyŏn wanjŏn ch'obo-iseyo?
do you have any experience, or are you a complete beginner?

보증금이 … -입니다
pojŭnggŭm-i … -imnida
there is a deposit of …

보험을 드셔야 해요. 보험료는 … -이에요
pohŏm-ŭl tŭshyŏya haeyo. pohŏmnyo-nŭn … -ieyo
insurance is compulsory and costs …

HIKING

Expressing yourself

are there any hiking paths around here?
이 근처에 하이킹 코스 있어요?
i kŭnch'ŏ-e haik'ing k'osŭ issŏyo?

can you recommend any good walks in the area?
이 근처에 좋은 산책 코스 있어요?
i kŭnch'ŏ-e choŭn sanch'aek k'osŭ issŏyo?

I've heard there's a nice walk by the lake
호수 근처에 좋은 산책로가 있다고 들었는데요
hosu kŭnch'ŏ-e choŭn sanch'aengno-ga ittago tŭrŏnnundeyo

we're looking for a short walk somewhere round here
이 근처에 간단한 산책로를 찾고 있어요?
i kŭnch'ŏ-e kandanhan sanch'aengno-rŭl ch'akko issŏyo?

can I hire hiking boots?
등산화 빌릴 수 있어요?
tŭngsanhwa pillil su issŏyo?

how long does the hike take?
등산이 얼마나 걸려요?
tŭngsan-i ŏlmana kŏllyŏyo?

is it very steep?
길이 아주 험해요?
kil-i aju hŏmhaeyo?

do you have a map?
지도 있어요?
chido issŏyo?

where's the start of the path?
등산로 입구가 어디에요?
tŭngsanno ipku-ga ŏdi-eyo?

is the path waymarked?
등산로에 표시가 있어요?
tŭngsanno p'yoshi-ga issŏyo?

is it a circular path?
순환코스에요?
sunhwan-k'osŭ-eyo?

Understanding

평균 소요시간 *p'yŏnggyun soyoshigan*   average duration *(of walk)*

휴식시간 포함해서 대강 세 시간어에요
hyushik-shigan pohamhaesŏ taegang se shigan-ieyo
it's about a three-hour walk including rest stops

방수 자캣하고 등산화를 가지고 오세요
pangsu chak'et-hago tŭngsanhwa-rŭl kajigo oseyo
bring a waterproof jacket and some walking shoes

SKIING AND SNOWBOARDING

Expressing yourself

I'd like to hire skis, poles and boots
스키하고 폴대하고 스키 부츠를 빌리고 싶어요
sŭk'i-hago p'oldae-hago sŭk'i puch'ŭ-rŭl pilligo ship'oyo

I'd like to hire a snowboard
스노우보드를 빌리고 싶어요
sŭnou-bodŭ-rŭl pilligo ship'ŏyo

they're too big/small
너무 커요／작아요
nŏmu k'ŏyo/chagayo

a day pass
일일 사용권
iril sayonggwon

I'm a complete beginner
완전 초보에요
wanjŏn ch'obo-eyo

Understanding

리프트 *rip'ŭtŭ*	chair lift
리프트 승차권 *rip'ŭtŭ sŭngch'agwon*	lift pass
스키 리프트 *sŭk'i rip'ŭtŭ*	ski lift
티-바 리프트 *t'i-ba rip'ŭtŭ*	T-bar, button lift

OTHER SPORTS

Expressing yourself

where can we hire bikes?
어디서 자전거 빌릴 수 있어요?
ŏdisŏ chajŏngŏ pillil su issŏyo?

are there any cycle paths?
자전거 타는 길 있어요?
chajŏngŏ t'anŭn kil issŏyo?

where can we play football/tennis/pool/badminton?
어디서 축구/테니스/포켓볼/배드민턴 할 수 있어요?
ŏdisŏ ch'ukku/t'enisŭ/p'ok'et-pol/paedŭmintŏn hal su issŏyo?

which team do you support?
어느 팀을 응원하세요?
ŏnŭ t'im-ŭl ŭngwonhaseyo?

I support ...
… 응원해요
… ŭngwonhaeyo

is there an open-air swimming pool?
야외 수영장 있어요?
yawe suyŏngjang issŏyo?

I've never been diving before
다이빙 해 본 적이 없어요
taibing hae pon chŏk-i ŏpsŏyo

can we hire rackets?
라켓 빌릴 수 있어요?
rak'et pillil su issŏyo?

where are the showers/changing rooms?
샤워실/탈의실이 어디에요?
shyawo/t'aruishil-i ŏdi-eyo?

I'd like to take beginners' sailing lessons
초보자용 요트 레슨을 받고 싶어요
ch'obochayong resŭn-ŭl pakko ship'ŏyo

I go for a run every morning
매일 아침 달리기 해요
maeil ach'im talligi haeyo

Understanding

역 가까이에 공용 테니스 코트가 있어요
yŏk kakkai-e kongyong t'enisŭ k'ot'ŭ-ga issŏyo
there's a public tennis court not far from the station

테니스 코트 사용중이에요
t'enisŭ k'ot'ŭ sayong-jung-ieyo
the tennis court's occupied

승마 처음이에요?
sŭngma ch'ŏŭm-ieyo?
is this the first time you've been horse-riding?

수영할 수 있어요?
suyŏnghal su issŏyo?
can you swim?

라커 열쇠가 있어야 돼요
rak'ŏ yŏlse-ga issŏya twaeyo
you'll need a key for the lockers

농구 할 줄 아세요?
nonggu hal chul aseyo?
do you play basketball?

INDOOR GAMES

Expressing yourself

shall we have a game of cards/chess?
카드 게임/체스 할까요?
k'adŭ keim/ch'esŭ halkkayo?

does anyone know any good card games?
누가 재미있는 카드 게임 아세요?
nuga jaemi-innŭn k'adŭ keim aseyo?

it's your turn
거기 차례에요
kŏgi ch'are-eyo

Understanding

체스 할 줄 아세요?
ch'esŭ hal chul aseyo?
do you know how to play chess?

당구 한번 할까요?
tanggu han-bŏn halkkayo?
shall we have a game of pool?

카드 있어요?
k'adŭ issŏyo?
do you have a pack of cards?

Some informal expressions

숨이 차서 죽겠어요 *sum-i ch'asŏ chukkessŏyo* I'm exhausted and out of breath

틈이 없네요 *t'ŭm-i ŏmneyo* there's no chink (in your armour) (said when your opponent is playing well)

그냥 죽여라 *kŭnyang chugyŏra* why don't you just kill me! (said to your opponent when you are getting beaten decisively)

SHOPPING

South Korea, and Seoul in particular, offers excellent opportunities for shopping. Fashion, antiques and electronics are usually high up on most people's shopping itineraries.

Shopping districts in Seoul include the markets at 남대문 *Namdaemun* and 동대문 *Dongdaemun*, the bustling fashion stores of 명동 *Myeong-dong*, the antiques market of 장안평 *Janganpyeong*, the antiques and art shops of 인사동 *Insa-dong* and the electronics market at 용산 *Yongsan*.

Although prices are fixed at department stores and other shops, they are often negotiable at markets. Discounts are more likely to be given if you are buying more than one item.

Some informal expressions

쇼핑광이에요 *shyop'ing-gwang-ieyo* (I am) shopping mad!
바가지 썼어요 *pagaji ssŏssŏyo* (I) got ripped off
말도 안 되는 가격이에요 *mal-do an twe-nŭn kagyŏk-ieyo* that's a ridiculous price!
덤이에요 *tŏm-ieyo* I'll throw this one in for free

The basics

bakery	빵집 *ppangjip*, 제과점 *chegwajŏm*
bookshop	책방 *ch'aekpang*, 서점 *sŏjŏm*
butcher's	정육점 *chŏngyukchŏm*
cash desk	계산대 *kesandae*
cheap	싸요 *ssayo*
checkout	정산 *chŏngsan*
clothes	옷 *ot*, 의류 *uiryu*
department store	백화점 *paek'wajŏm*
expensive	비싸요 *pissayo*
gram	그램 *kŭraem*

greengrocer's	청과물 *chŏnggwamul*
kilo	킬로 *k'illo*
present	선물 *sŏnmul*
price	값 *kap*, 가격 *kagyŏk*
receipt	영수증 *yŏngsujŭng*
refund	환불 *hwambul*
sales	(바겐)세일 *(pagen) seil*
sales assistant	점원 *chŏmwŏn*
shop	가게 *kage*
shopping centre	쇼핑센터 *shyop'ing sent'ŏ*
souvenir	기념품 *kinyŏmp'um*
supermarket	슈퍼(마켓) *sup'ŏ(mak'et)*
vending machine	자동판매기 *chadongp'anmaegi*
to buy	사요 *sayo*
to pay	돈 내요 *ton naeyo*
to sell	팔아요 *p'arayo*

Expressing yourself

is there a supermarket near here?
이 근처에 슈퍼(마켓) 있어요?
i kŭnch'ŏ-e sup'ŏ(mak'et) issŏyo?

where can I buy cigarettes?
담배 어디서 팔아요?
tambae ŏdi-sŏ p'arayo?

I'd like ...
... 주세요
... chuseyo

I'm looking for ...
... 찾고 있는데요
... chak-ko innŭndeyo

do you sell ...?
... 팔아요?
... p'arayo?

can you order it for me?
주문할 수 있어요?
chumunhal su issŏyo?

do you know where I might find some ...?
... 어디서 파는지 아세요?
... ŏdisŏ p'anŭnji aseyo?

how much is this?
이 거 얼마에요?
i kŏ ŏlma-eyo?

I'll take it
그 거 주세요
kŭ kŏ chuseyo

I haven't got much money
돈이 많이 없어요
ton-i mani ŏpsŏyo

I haven't got enough money
돈이 충분하지 않아요
ton-i ch'ungbunhaji anayo

that's everything, thanks
그 게 전부에요. 감사합니다
ku ke chŏmbu-eyo. kamsahamnida

can I have a (plastic) bag?
(비닐) 봉투 주세요
(pinil) pongt'u chuseyo

I think you've made a mistake with my change
잔돈 계산이 틀린 거 같은데요
chandon kesan-i t'ŭllin kŏ kat'ŭndeyo

Understanding

… **시부터 … 시까지 영업** *… shi-put'ŏ … shi-kkaji yŏngŏp*	open from … to …
일요일 휴업 *ilyoil hyuŏp*	closed Sundays
특별 할인 *tŭkpyŏl harin*	special offer
세일 *seil*	sales

다른 사고 싶은 거 있으세요?
tarŭn sago ship'ŭn kŏ issŭseyo?
will there be anything else?

봉투 필요하세요?
pongt'u p'ilyohaseyo?
would you like a bag?

PAYING

Expressing yourself

where do I pay?
돈은 어디서 내요?
ton-ŭn ŏdi-sŏ naeyo?

how much do I owe you?
얼마에요?
ŏlma-eyo?

could you write it down for me, please?
써 주시겠어요?
ssŏ chushigessŏyo?

can I pay by credit card?
신용카드 받아요?
shinyong-k'adŭ padayo?

I'll pay in cash
현금으로 낼게요
hyŏnggŭm-ŭro naelkkeyo

I'm sorry, I haven't got any change
미안하지만, 잔돈이 없어요
mianhajiman, chandon-i ŏpsŏyo

can I have a receipt?
영수증 주세요
yŏngsujŭng chuseyo

Understanding

여기서 내세요
yŏgi-sŏ naeseyo
please pay here

계산대에서 계산하세요
kesandae-esŏ kesanhaseyo
pay at the cash desk

지불은 뭘로 하시겠어요?
chibul-ŭn mŏl-lo hashigessŏyo?
how would you like to pay?

잔돈 없으세요?
chandon ŏpsŭseyo?
do you have anything smaller?

신분증 있으세요?
shimbunjŭng issŭseyo?
have you got any ID?

여기 사인해 주세요
yŏgi sainhae chuseyo
could you sign here, please?

FOOD

Expressing yourself

where can I buy food around here?
이 근처에 음식은 어디서 팔아요?
i kŭnch'ŏ-e ŭmshik-ŭn ŏdi-sŏ p'arayo?

is there a market?
시장 있어요?
shijang issŏyo?

is there a bakery around here?
이 근처에 제과점 있어요?
i kŭnch'ŏ-e chegwajŏm issŏyo?

I'm looking for fruit and vegetables
과일하고 야채를 찾고 있는데요
kwail-hago yach'ae-rŭl ch'akko innŭndeyo

I'd like five packs of kimchi
김치 다섯 봉지 주세요
kimch'i tasŏt pongji chuseyo

I'd like some ham and some cheese
햄하고 치즈 좀 주세요
haem-hago ch'ijŭ chom chuseyo

it's for four people
사 인분이에요
sa impun-ieyo

about 300 grams
삼백 그램 정도
sam-paek kŭraem chŏngdo

a kilo of meat, please
고기 일 킬로 주세요
kogi il k'illo chuseyo

ten apples, please
사과 열 개 주세요
sagwa yŏl kae chuseyo

a bit less/more
좀 덜／더
chom tŏl/tŏ

can I taste it?
먹어 봐도 돼요?
mŏgŏ pa-do twaeyo?

does it travel well?
가지고 여행해도 돼요?
kajigo yŏhaenghaedo twaeyo

Understanding

지방 특산품 *chibang t'ŭksanp'um*	local specialities
유기농 *yuginong*	organic
수제품 *sujep'um*	homemade
유통기한 *yut'onggihan*	best before

매일 한 시까지 시장이 열려요
maeil han shi-kkaji shijang-i yŏllyŏyo
there's a market every day until 1pm

저 골목에 늦게까지 여는 청과물 가게가 있어요
chŏ kolmok-e nŭkke-kkaji yŏ-nŭn ch'ŏnggwamul kage-ga issŏyo
there's a grocer's just on the corner that's open late

CLOTHES

Expressing yourself

I'm looking for the menswear section
신사복 매장이 어디에요?
shinsabok maejang-i ŏdi-eyo?

no thanks, I'm just looking
아니요, 그냥 보는 거에요
aniyo, kŭnyang po-nŭn kŏ-eyo

can I try it on?
입어 봐도 돼요?
ibŏ pado twaeyo?

I'd like to try the one in the window
진열장에 있는 거 입어 보고 싶어요
chinyŏljang-e innŭn kŏ ibŏ pogo ship'ŏyo

I take a size 270 mm (in shoes)
제 사이즈는 이백칠십이에요
che saijŭ-nŭn i-paek-ch'il-ship-ieyo

where are the changing rooms?
탈의실이 어디에요?
t'aluishil-i ŏdi-eyo?

it doesn't fit
안 맞아요
an majayo

it's too big/small
너무 커요／작아요
nŏmu k'ŏyo/chagayo

do you have it in another colour?
다른 색깔 있어요?
tarŭn saekkal issŏyo?

do you have it in a smaller/bigger size?
작은／큰 사이즈 있어요?
chagŭn/k'ŭn saijŭ issŏyo?

do you have them in red?
빨간 색 있어요?
ppalgan saek issŏyo?

yes, that's fine, I'll take them
네, 좋아요. 그 거 주세요
ne, choayo. kŭ kŏ chuseyo

no, I don't like it
아니요, 그 거 싫어요
aniyo, kŭ kŏ shilŏyo

I'll think about it
생각 좀 해 볼게요
saenggak chom hae polkkeyo

SHOPPING

I'd like to return this, it doesn't fit
이 거 안 맞아서 반품하고 싶어요
i kŏ an majasŏ panp'umhago ship'ŏyo

this ... has a hole in it, can I get a refund?
여기 구멍이 있는데, 환불해 주세요
yŏgi kumŏng-i innŭnde, hwambulhae chuseyo

Understanding

탈의실 *t'aluishil* — changing rooms

세일 상품은 반품 안 됩니다 — sale items cannot be returned
seil sangp'um-ŭn panp'um an twemnida

일요일 영업 *ilyoil yŏngŏp* — open Sunday
아동복 *adongbok* — children's clothes
숙녀복 *sungnyŏbok* — ladieswear
신사복 *shinsabok* — menswear
란제리 *ranjeri* — lingerie

어서 오세요. 뭘 찾으세요?
ŏsŏ oseyo. mŏl ch'ajŭseyo?
hello, can I help you?

파란 색하고 검은 색 밖에 없어요
p'aran saek-hago kŏmŭn saek pakk-e ŏpsŏyo
we only have it in blue or black

그 사이즈는 다 팔렸어요
kŭ saijŭ-nŭn ta p'allyŏssŏyo
we don't have any left in that size

잘 어울려요
chal ŏullyŏyo
it suits you

딱 맞아요
ttak majayo
it's a good fit

안 맞으면 교환해 드려요
an majŭmyŏn kyohwanhae tŭryŏyo
you can bring it back if it doesn't fit

SOUVENIRS AND PRESENTS

Expressing yourself

I'm looking for a present to take home
선물을 사고 싶어요
sŏmmul-ŭl sago ship'ŏyo

do you have anything made locally?
이 지방 특산품 있어요?
i chibang t'ŭksanp'um issŏyo?

I'd like something that's easy to transport
간편하게 가지고 갈 수 있는 거 사고 싶어요
kanp'yŏnhage kajigo kal su innŭn kŏ sago ship'ŏyo

it's for a little girl of four
네 살짜리 여자 아이 거에요
ne sal-tchari yŏja ai kŏ-eyo

could you gift-wrap it for me?
예쁘게 포장해 주세요
yeppŭge p'ojanghae chuseyo

Understanding

목제품/은제품/금제품   made of wood/silver/gold
  mokchep'um/ŭnjep'um/kŭmjep'um

수제품 *sujep'um*   handmade
전통 공예품 *chŏnt'ong kongep'um*   traditionally made product
도자기 *tojagi*   pottery

얼마 정도 예상하세요?
ŏlma chŏngdo yesanghaseyo?
how much do you want to spend?

선물용이에요?
sŏmmulyong-ieyo?
is it for a present?

이 지방 특산품이에요
i chibang t'ŭksanp'um-ieyo
it's typical of the region

SHOPPING

97

PHOTOS

Developing film and purchasing photography equipment are both inexpensive in South Korea. If you are looking to buy cameras or other gadgets, the Yongsan electronics market in Seoul is the place to head. Prices are cheap and the vendors will offer discounts, if asked.

In North Korea, film and other equipment are available, but tend to be expensive. There are reports of tourists in North Korea being prevented from photographing scenes of poverty and so on that could show the country in a bad light.

The basics

battery	건전지	*kŏnjŏnji*
black and white	흑백	*hŭkpaek*
camera	카메라	*k'amera*
CD	씨디	*ssidi (CD)*
colour	칼라	*k'alla*
copy	복사	*poksa*
digital camera	디지탈 카메라	*tijit'al k'amera*
disposable camera	일회용 카메라	*ilhwayong k'amera*
exposure	노출	*noch'ul*
film	필름	*p'illŭm*
flash	플래쉬	*p'ŭllaeshi*
glossy	광택	*kwangt'aek*
matte	무광택	*mugwangt'aek*
memory card	메모리 카드	*memori k'adŭ*
negative	원판	*wonpan*
passport photo	여권사진	*yŏgwonsajin*
photo booth	즉석 사진실	*chŭksŏk sajinshil*
reprint	복사	*poksa*
slide	슬라이드	*sŭllaidŭ*
to get photos developed	사진을 현상해요	*sajin-ŭl hyŏnsanghaeyo*
to take a photo/photos	사진을 찍어요	*sajin-ŭl tchikŏyo*

Expressing yourself

could you take a photo of us, please?
사진 좀 찍어 주시겠어요?
sajin com tchikŏ chusigessŏyo?

you just have to press this button
이 버튼만 누르세요
i pŏt'ŭn-man nurŭseyo

I'd like a 200 ASA colour film
아사 이백 (ASA 200) 칼라 필름 주세요
asa i-paek (ASA 200) k'alla p'illŭm chuseyo

do you have black and white films?
흑백 필름 있어요?
hŭkpaek p'illŭm issŏyo?

how much is it to develop a film of 36 photos?
삼십육방 필름 현상하는 데 얼마에요?
samshipyuk-pang p'illŭm hyŏnsanghanŭn te ŏlma-eyo?

I'd like to have this film developed
이 필름 현상해 주세요
i p'illŭm hyŏnsanghae chuseyo

I'd like extra copies of some of the photos
어떤 사진은 두 장씩 뽑아 주세요
ŏttŏn sajin-ŭn tu chang-ssik ppoba chuseyo

three copies of this one and two of this one
이 거 세 장씩, 그리고 이 거 두 장씩
i kŏ se chang-ssik, kŭligo i kŏ tu chang-ssik

can I print my digital photos here?
여기서 디지털 사진 프린트할 수 있어요?
yŏgi-sŏ tijit'ŏl sajin p'ŭrintŭ-hal su issŏyo?

can you put these photos on a CD for me?
이 사진들 씨디에 구울 수 있어요?
i sajin-dŭl ssidi-e ku-ul su issŏyo?

I've come to pick up my photos
사진 찾으러 왔어요
sajin ch'ajŭrŏ wassŏyo

99

I've got a problem with my camera
카메라에 문제가 있어요
k'amera-e munje-ga issŏyo

I don't know what it is
뭔지 모르겠어요
mŏnji morŭgessŏyo

the flash doesn't work
플래시가 고장났어요
p'ŭllaeshi-ga kojangnassŏyo

Understanding

한 시간 사진 현상
   han shigan sajin hyŏnsang

photos developed in one hour

일반 현상 *ilban hyŏnsang*

standard format

고속 현상 *kosok hyŏnsang*

express service

씨디 사진 *ssidi sajin*

photos on CD

아마 건전지는 다 쓴 거에요
ama kŏnjŏnji-nŭn ta ssŭn kŏ-eyyo
maybe the battery's dead

디지탈 사진을 프린트하는 기계가 있어요
tijit'al sajin-ŭl p'ŭrint'ŭ-hanŭn kige-ga issŏyo
we have a machine for printing digital photos

성함이 어떻게 되세요?
sŏngham-i ŏttŏke toyseyo
what's the name, please?

언제 필요하세요?
ŏnje p'iryo-kashigessŏyo?
when do you need them for?

한 시간 안에 현상할 수 있어요
han shigan an-e hyŏnsanghal su issŏyo
we can develop them in an hour

목요일 12시에 찾아가세요
mogyoil yŏl-tu-shi-e ch'aja-kaseyo
you can pick up your photos on Thursday at noon

South Korean won (원) are not readily available outside of South Korea, so you are best off waiting until you get off the plane before you think about changing money. Banks represent the best value for converting cash as well as travellers cheques. Cash machines are plentiful in the cities and can often be found in underground stations and convenience stores as well as banks. Most of these machines now accept international cards and have an English language option. Many of these machines (especially when in Korean mode) will ask you for the amount you wish to withdraw in units of 10,000 (만 *man*) won. For example, if you want to withdraw 200,000 won, you will need to select 20 만 (*man*). All except the smallest of shops and restaurants will accept credit cards, although be warned that this is sometimes limited to locally issued cards.

In surveys comparing the cost of living in major cities, Seoul is often listed as being amongst the most expensive places in the world. Such surveys, however, are often based around the needs of expats living in Western-style accommodation, eating Western food and sending their children to foreign schools. For the traveller, South Korea represents good value for money. Hotels, eating out and transportation are generally much cheaper than in the West.

The currency of North Korea is also called the *won*. Euros, dollars, pounds and yen can be changed into the local currency only at hotels.

The different denominations (South Korea)

Coins (동전 *dongjŏn*)

십원 *ship-won*	10 won
오십원 *o-ship-won*	50 won
백원 *paek-won*	100 won
오백원 *o-paek-won*	500 won

Notes (지폐 chip'e**)**

천원 chŏn-won	1,000 won
오천원 o-chŏn won	5,000 won
만원 man-won	10,000 won

"Cheques" (수표 sup'yo**)**

For large sums of money, South Koreans use a kind of bankers' cheque known as a sup'yo. These can come in fixed amounts – most commonly 100,000 won (십만원 ship-man-won) – and can also be made out in specific amounts. Sup'yo can be used like cash; however, you will normally be asked for ID.

If you are in Korea on a short pleasure trip, you are unlikely to encounter sup'yo. However, note that cash machines may ask you if you want the amount in cash (현금 hyŏngŭm) or sup'yo.

The basics

bank	은행 ŭnhaeng
bank account	은행 계좌 ŭnhaeng kejwa
banknote	지폐 chip'e
bureau de change	환전소 hwanjŏnso
cashpoint	현금 출납기 hyŏngŭm ch'ulnapki
change	잔돈 chandon
cheque	수표 sup'yo
coin	동전 tongjŏn
commission	수수료 susuryo
credit card	신용카드 shinyongk'adŭ
PIN (number)	비밀번호 pimilbŏnho
transfer	송금 songgŭm, 이체 ich'e
Travellers Cheques®	여행자 수표 yŏhaengja sup'yo
withdrawal	출금 ch'ulgŭ, 인출 inch'ul
to change	바꿔요 pakkwoyo, 환전해요 hwanjŏnhaeyo
to transfer	송금해요 songgŭmhaeyo, 이체해요 ich'ehaeyo
to withdraw	출금해요 ch'ulgŭmhaeyo, 인출해요 inch'ulhaeyo

Expressing yourself

where can I get some money changed?
어디서 환전해요?
ŏdisŏ hwanjŏnhaeyo?

are banks open on Saturdays?
토요일에 은행 열어요?
t'oyoil-e ŭnhaeng yŏlŏyo?

where can I find a cashpoint?
현금출납기 어디 있어요?
hyŏngŭmch'ulnapki ŏdi issŏyo?

I'd like to change £100
백 파운드 바꿔 주세요
paek paundŭ pakkwo chuseyo

what commission do you charge?
수수료가 얼마에요?
susuryo-ga ŏlma-eyo?

I'd like to transfer some money
돈을 송금해 주세요
ton-ŭl songgŭmhae chuseyo

I'd like to report the loss of my credit card
신용카드 분실 신고를 하고 싶어요
shinyongk'adŭ punshil shingo-rŭl hago ship'ŏyo

the cashpoint has swallowed my card
현금출납기가 제 카드를 먹었어요
hyŏnggumch'ulnapki-ga che k'adŭ-rŭl mŏgŏssŏyo

Understanding

카드를 넣어 주십시오
k'adŭ-rŭl nŏ-ŏ chushipshio
please insert your card

비밀번호를 입력해 주십시오
pimilbŏnho-rŭl imnyŏk'ae chushipshio
please enter your PIN number

원하는 금액을 입력하십시오
wonha-nŭn kŭmaek-ŭl imnyŏk'ashipshio
please select amount for withdrawal

출금표를 출력하시겠습니까?
ch'ulgump'yo-rul ch'ullyŏk'ashigessŭpnikka?
would you like a receipt?

고장/수리중
kojang/surijung
out of service

현금
hyŏngŭm
cash

수표
sup'yo
cheque

POST OFFICES

In South Korea, post offices are open from 9am to 6pm Monday to Friday and are recognizable by large red signs reading 우체국 (*uch'eguk* "post office"). Regular airmail letters to Western Europe normally take less than one week to arrive. Post offices also offer inexpensive packing services for sending parcels.

In North Korea, the major tourist hotels offer postal services.

The basics

airmail	항공우편 *hanggong up'yŏn*
envelope	봉투 *pongt'u*
letter	편지 *p'yŏnji*
mail	우편 *up'yŏn*
parcel	소포 *sop'o*
post	우편 *up'yŏn*
postbox	우체통 *uch'et'ong*
postcard	엽서 *yŏpsŏ*
postcode	우편번호 *up'yŏn-pŏnho*
post office	우체국 *uch'eguk*
stamp	우표 *up'yo*
to post	우송해요 *usonghaeyo*
to send	보내요 *ponaeyo*
to write	써요 *ssŏyo*

Expressing yourself

is there a post office around here?
이 근처에 우체국 있어요?
i kŭnjŏ-e uch'eguk issŏyo?

is there a postbox near here?
이 근처에 우체통 있어요?
i kŭnjŏ-e uch'et'ong issŏyo?

is the post office open on Saturdays?
토요일에 우체국 열어요?
t'oyoil-e uch'eguk yŏlŏyo?

what time does the post office close?
몇 시에 우체국 닫아요?
myŏ shi-e uch'eguk tadayo?

do you sell stamps?
우표 팔아요?
up'yo p'alayo?

I'd like ... stamps for the UK, please
영국 가는 우표 … 개 주세요
yŏngguk ka-nŭn up'yo ... gae chuseyyo

how long will it take to arrive?
얼마나 걸려요?
ŏlmana kŏllyŏyo?

where can I buy envelopes?
봉투 어디서 팔아요?
pongt'u ŏdisŏ p'alayo?

is there any post for me?
저한테 온 편지 있어요?
chŏ-hant'e on p'yŏnji issŏyo?

Understanding

깨지기 쉬움	*kkaejigi shwium*	fragile
취급주의	*ch'wigŭpchu-ui*	handle with care
등기 우편	*tŭnggi up'yŏn*	registered mail
빠른 우편	*pparŭn up'yŏn*	swift mail
받는 사람	*pan-nŭn saram*	recipient
보내는 사람	*ponaenŭn saram*	sender

삼 일에서 오 일 정도 걸려요
sam il-esŏ o il chŏngdo kŏllyŏyo
it'll take between three and five days

INTERNET CAFÉS AND E-MAIL

South Korea has some of the highest rates of Internet use and broadband access in the world. Broadband connections are also amongst the fastest with 100Mb coverage being widespread.

In Seoul and the major cities, Internet cafes can literally be found on every street corner and are cheap too. Most of these come in the guise of the PC방 *PC-bang* (literally "PC room"), which are predominantly used by computer-game players rather than web surfers. Of course, there is nothing to stop you using these places to check your e-mail, but expect to be surrounded by gamers rather than bloggers.

Korean keyboards can be used to type both Korean and English. To toggle between the two, just hit the specially marked alt key directly to the right of the space bar.

In North Korea, Internet access is highly restricted. Instead of being hooked up to the World Wide Web, computers are hooked up to an intranet whereby only domestic web pages can be accessed.

The basics

at sign	골뱅이 *kolbaengi*
e-mail address	이메일 주소 *imeil chuso*
Internet café	인터넷 카페 *int'ŏnet kap'e* (Western-style Internet café); PC방 *PC-pang* (Korean style "PC room", mainly used by gamers)
key	키 *k'i*
keyboard	키보드 *k'ibodŭ*
to copy	복사하기 *poksahagi*
to cut	잘라내기 *challanaegi*
to delete	삭제하기 *sakchehagi*
to download	다운로드 *taunrodŭ*

to e-mail	이메일 해요 *imeil haeyo*
to e-mail someone	이메일을 보내요 *imeil-ul ponaeyo*
to paste	붙이기 *puch'igi*
to receive	수신하기 *sushinhagi*
to save	저장하기 *chŏjanghagi*
to send an e-mail	이메일을 보내요 *imeil-ul ponaeyo*

Expressing yourself

is there an Internet café near here?
이 근처에 PC방 있어요?
i kŭnch'ŏ-e PC-bang issŏyo?

do you have an e-mail address?
이메일 주소 있어요?
imeil chuso issŏyo?

how do I get online?
어떻게 인터넷에 접속할 수 있어요?
ŏttŏge intŏnes-e chŏpsokhal su issŏyo?

I'd just like to check my e-mails
제 이메일을 체크하고 싶어요
che imeil-ŭl ch'ekŭ-hago ship'ŏyo

would you mind helping me, I'm not sure what to do
어떻게 하는지 모르겠는데, 도와 주세요
ŏttŏge hanŭnji morŭgennŭnde, towa chuseyo

I can't find the at sign on this keyboard
골뱅이 표시를 못 찾겠어요
kolbaengi p'yoshi-rŭl mot ch'atkessŏyo

it's not working
작동 안 해요
chaktong an haeyo

there's something wrong with the computer, it's frozen
컴퓨터가 고장 났나 봐요. 먹통이에요
k'ŏmp'yutŏ-ga kojang nanna payo. mŏkt'ong-ieyo

how much will it be for half an hour?
삼십 분에 얼마에요?
samship pun-e ŏlmaeyo?

when do I pay?
(돈은) 언제 내야 돼요?
ton-ŭn ŏnje naeya twaeyo?

Understanding

받은 편지함 *padŭn p'yŏnjiham* inbox
보낸 편지함 *ponaen p'yŏnjiham* outbox

이십분 정도 기다리셔야 돼요
iship-pun chongdo kidalisyŏya twaeyo
you'll have to wait for 20 minutes or so

모르는 것이 있으면 물어 보세요
morŭnŭn kosh-i issŭmyŏn murŏ poseyo
just ask if you're not sure what to do

이 패스워드로 로그인 하세요
i paesŭwodŭ-ro rogŭ-in haseyo
just enter this password to log on

시간이 다 됐어요
shigan-i ta twaessŏyo
I'm afraid your time has run out

INTERNET CAFÉS, E-MAIL

109

TELEPHONE

(i)

In South Korea, public phones are widespread and can often be found in underground stations or outside local stores as well as in streetside phone boxes. Although some public phones take coins, other require phonecards (전화 카드 *chŏnhwa-k'adŭ*). These can easily be bought from convenience stores or news stands.

Since South Korea (along with neighbouring Japan) does not use a GSM system, most overseas mobile phones are not compatible with local networks. However, mobiles can be hired at reasonable rates from various locations, including Incheon International Airport. Mobile technology tends to be a step ahead of Western Europe, so expect a fancy new handset!

To dial overseas from South Korea, dial 001 followed by the international dialling code to place the call through Korea Telecom. Other service providers also exist, each using a different number (002, 007, etc).

In North Korea, some large hotels offer international direct dialling calls. Otherwise, you will need to book the call through the operator.

The basics

answering machine	자동응답기 *chadongŭngdapgi*
call	전화 *chŏnhwa*
directory enquiries	(전화)번호 안내 *(chŏnhwa)pŏnho annae*
hello	여보세요 *yŏboseyo*
international call	국제전화 *kukche-chŏnhwa*
local call	시내전화 *sinae-chŏnhwa*
message	메세지 *meseji*
mobile	휴대전화 *hyudae-chŏnhwa*, 핸드폰 *haendŭp'on*
national call	시외전화 *siwe-chŏnhwa*
phone	전화 *chŏnhwa*
phone book	전화번호부 *chŏnhwa-bŏnhobu*

phone box	공중전화 kongjung-chŏnhwa
phone call	전화 chŏnhwa
phone number	전화번호 chŏnhwa-bŏnho
phonecard	전화카드 chŏnhwa-k'adŭ
ringtone	착신음 ch'akshinŭm
to call someone	전화해요 chŏnhwahaeyo

where can I buy a phonecard?
전화카드 어디서 팔아요?
chŏnhwa-k'adŭ ŏdisŏ p'alayo?

a 5,000-won phonecard, please
오천원짜리 전화 카드 주세요
o-ch'ŏn-won-tchari chŏnhwa-k'adŭ chuseyo

I'd like to make a reverse-charge call
콜렉트 콜 통화하고 싶어요
k'ollekt'ŭ k'ol t'onghwa-hago ship'ŏyo

is there a phone box near here, please?
여기 공중전화 있어요?
yŏgi kongjung-chŏnhwa issŏyo?

can I plug my phone in here to recharge it?
여기서 휴대전화 충전해도 돼요?
yŏgisŏ hyudae-chŏnhwa ch'ungjŏnhaedo twaeyo?

do you have a mobile number?
휴대전화 번호 있어요?
hyudae-chŏnhwa pŏnho issŏyo?

where can I contact you?
어디로 연락하면 될까요?
ŏdi-ro yŏllak'amyŏn twelkkayo?

did you get my message?
제 메세지 받으셨어요?
che meseji padŭshyŏssŏyo?

TELEPHONE

Understanding

지금 거신 전화번호는 없는 번호이거나 잘못된 번호이니 다시 확인하시고 걸어 주세요

chigŭm kŏshin chŏnhwa-bŏnho-nŭn ŏmnŭn bŏnho-igŏna chalmodwen bŏnho-ini tashi hwaginhashigo kŏrŏ chuseyo

the number you have dialled has not been recognized

별표를/우물 정자를 눌러 주세요

pyŏlp'yo-rŭl/umul chŏngja-rŭl nullŏ chuseyo

please press the star/hash key

MAKING A CALL

Expressing yourself

hello, this is David Brown (speaking)
여보세요. 저 데이빗 브라운입니다
yŏboseyo, chŏ david brown-imnida

hello, could I speak to ..., please?
여보세요. … 좀 바꿔 주세요
yŏboseyo, ... chom pakkwo chuseyo

hello, is that Mr Kim?
여보세요. 김선생님이세요?
yŏboseyo, kim-sŏnsaengnim-iseyo?

do you speak English?
영어 하세요?
yŏngŏ haseyo?

could you speak more slowly, please?
좀 더 천천히 말씀해 주세요
chom tŏ ch'ŏnch'ŏnhi malssŭm-hae chuseyo

I can't hear you, could you speak up, please?
잘 안 들려요. 크게 말씀해 주세요
chal an tŭllyŏyo. k'ŭge malssŭm-hae chuseyo

could you tell him/her I called?
제가 전화했다고 좀 전해 주세요
che-ga chŏnhwa-haettago chom chŏnhae chuseyo

could you ask him/her to call me back?
저한테 전화해 달라고 전해 주세요
chŏ-hant'e chŏnhwa-hae tallago chŏnhae chuseyo

I'll call back later
나중에 다시 전화할게요
najung-e tashi chŏnhwa-halkkeyo

my name is … and my number is …
제 이름은 … 이고, 전화번호는 … 이에요
che irŭm-ŭn …-igo chŏnhwa-bŏnho-nŭn …-ieyo

do you know when he/she might be available?
언제쯤 통화 가능할까요?
ŏnje-tchŭm t'onghwa kanŭnghalkkayo?

thank you, goodbye
감사합니다, 안녕히 계세요
kamsahamnida, annyŏnghi keseyo

Understanding

누구세요?
nuguseyo?
who's calling?

전화 잘못 거셨어요
chŏnhwa chalmot kŏshyŏssŏyo
you've got the wrong number

지금 없는데요
chigŭm ŏmnŭndeyo
he's/she's not here at the moment

메세지 남기시겠어요?
meseji namgishigessŏyo?
do you want to leave a message?

전화 왔었다고 전해 드릴게요
chŏnhwa wassŏttago chŏnhae tŭrilkkeyo
I'll tell him/her you called

전화하라고 전해 드릴게요
chŏnhwa-harago chŏnhae tŭrilkkeyo
I'll ask him/her to call you back

잠깐 기다리세요
chamkkan kidariseyo
hold on

바꿔 드릴게요
pakkwo tŭrilkkeyo
I'll just hand you over to him/her

PROBLEMS

Expressing yourself

I don't know the code
국번을 모르는데요
kukpŏn-ŭl morŭnŭndeyo

it's engaged
통화중이에요
t'onghwa-chung-ieyo

there's no reply
전화 안 받는데요
chŏnhwa an pannŭndeyo

I couldn't get through
연결이 안 되는데요
yŏngyŏl-i an twenŭndeyo

I don't have much credit left on my phone
전화에 돈이 얼마 안 남았어요
chŏnhwa-e ton-i ŏlma an namassŏyo

we're about to get cut off
이제 곧 끊길거에요
ije kot kkŭnk'ilgŏeyo

the reception's really bad
수신상태가 안 좋아요
sushinsangt'ae-ga an choayo

I can't get a signal
안테나가 안 잡혀요
ant'ena-ga an chap'yŏyo

Understanding

잘 안 들려요
chal an tŭllyŏyo
I can hardly hear you

잡음이 많아요
chabŭm-i manayo
it's a bad line

Ending the conversation

These are some common expressions used by Korean speakers when
they want to end the telephone conversation and hang up.

끊을게요 *kkŭnŭlgeyo* "I'm going to hang up"

들어가세요 *tŭrŏgaseyo* this literally means "go inside", but is used to
mean "goodbye" when on the phone

네 *ney*, 예 *yey* "yes" – most conversations are ended by both speakers
saying "yes", sometimes two or three times!

TELEPHONE

HEALTH

ℹ️

Most chemists (약국 *yakkuk* – often signposted just 약) open from 9am until late evening, often 9pm. Despite these long opening hours, getting medicine at night is very difficult. Even in Seoul, A&E may be the only option. Expect the range and strength of medicine that chemists are allowed to dispense to be superior to what you can get at home.

Korea has no GP system. Patients choose a specialist clinic based on their ailment and go straight there. For most everyday illnesses, go to the 내과 *naegwa* (internal medicine clinic). For cuts, sprains and so on, try the 외과 *wegwa* (external medicine clinic). Other clinics you may need include the 이비인후과 *ibiinhugwa* (ear, nose and throat specialist), 피부과 *p'ibugwa* (dermatologist) and 산부인과 *sabuingwa* (gynaecologist).

As well as Western medicine, oriental medicines are also commonly dispensed at chemists. Oriental medical clinics known as 한의원 *haniwon* are also widespread.

Note that most doctors and medical staff have been trained using textbooks written in English. Therefore, although not all will be able to speak English as such, most will know the English names for ailments and medicines.

The basics

allergy	알레르기 *allerŭgi*
ambulance	구급차 *kugŭpch'a*
aspirin	아스피린 *asŭp'irin*
blood	피 *pi*, 혈액 *hyŏraek*
broken	부러졌어요 *purŏjyŏssŏyo*
casualty (department)	응급실 *ŭnggŭpshil*
chemist's	약국 *yakkuk*
condom	콘돔 *kondom*
dentist	치과 *ch'igwa*

diarrhoea	설사 *sŏlsa*
doctor	의사 *uisa*
food poisoning	식중독 *shikchungdok*
gynaecologist	산부인과 *sanbu-ingwa*
hospital	병원 *pyŏngwon*
infection	감염 *kamyŏn*
medicine	약 *yak*
operation	수술 *susul*
painkiller	진통제 *chint'ongje*
periods	생리 *saengni*
plaster	반창고 *panch'anggo*
rash	발진 *paljin*
spot	반점 *panjŏm*
sunburn	햇볕 화상 *haeppyŏt hwasang*
surgical spirit	소독용 알코올 *sodok-yong alk'ool*
tablet	알약 *al-lyak*
temperature	열이 나요 *yŏr-i nayo*
tests	테스트 *t'esŭt'ŭ*
vaccination	예방접종 *yebangjŏpjong*
x-ray	엑스레이 *eksŭrei*
to disinfect	소독해요 *sodok'aeyo*
to faint	기절해요 *kijŏlhaeyo*
to vomit	토해요 *t'ohaeyo*

Expressing yourself

does anyone have an aspirin/a tampon/a plaster, by any chance?
혹시 아스피린/생리대/반창고 있어요?
hokshi asŭp'irin/saengnidae/panch'anggo issŏyo?

I need to go to the doctor's
병원에 가야 되요
pyŏngwon-e kaya twaeyo

where can I find a doctor's surgery?
병원이 어디에요?
pyongwon-i ŏdi-eyo?

I'd like to make an appointment for today
오늘 진찰 예약하고 싶어요
onŭl chinch'al yeyak'ago ship'ŏyo

as soon as possible
가능한한 빨리
kanŭnghanhan ppalli

no, it doesn't matter
아니요, 괜찮아요
aniyo, kwaench'anayo

can you send an ambulance to ...
… 에 구급차 보내 주세요
… -e kugŭpch'a ponae chuseyo

I've broken my glasses
안경이 깨졌어요
angyŏng-i kkaejyŏssŏyo

I've lost a contact lens
콘택트 렌즈를 잃어버렸어요
k'ont'eakt'ŭ renjŭ irŏpŏryŏssŏyo

Understanding

병원 pyŏngwon	doctor's surgery
처방전 ch'ŏbangjŏn	prescription
용급실 ŭnggŭpshil	casualty department

목요일까지 예약이 다 찼어요
mogyoil-kkaji yeyak-i ta ch'assŏyo
there are no available appointments until Thursday

금요일 오후 두 시 좋아요?
kŭmyoil ohu tu shi choayo?
is Friday at 2pm OK?

AT THE DOCTOR'S OR THE HOSPITAL

Expressing yourself

I have an appointment with Dr ...
… 의사 선생님하고 약속이 있어요
… uisa sŏnsaengnim-hago yaksok-i issŏyo

I don't feel very well
몸이 좀 아파요
mom-i chom ap'ayo

I feel very weak
기운이 없어요
kiun-i ŏpsŏyo

I don't know what it is
뭔지 잘 모르겠어요
mŏnji chal morŭgessŏyo

I've been bitten/stung by ...
… 한테 물렸어요
... hant'e mullyŏssŏyo

I've got a headache
머리가 아파요
mŏri-ga ap'ayo

I've got toothache/stomachache
이가／배가 아파요
i-ga/pae-ga ap'ayo

I've got a sore throat
목이 아파요
mok-i ap'ayo

my back hurts
허리가 아파요
hŏri-ga ap'ayo

it hurts
아파요
ap'ayo

it hurts here
여기가 아파요
yŏgi-ga ap'ayo

I feel sick
토할 거 같아요
t'ohal kŏ kat'ayo

it's got worse
더 심해졌어요
tŏ shimhaejyŏssŏyo

it's been three days
삼 일 됐어요
sam il twaessŏyo

it started last night
어제 밤부터 시작됐어요
ŏje pam-put'ŏ shijak-twaessŏyo

it's never happened to me before
처음이에요
ch'ŏŭm-ieyo

I've got a temperature
열이 나요
yŏl-i nayo

I have asthma
천식이 있어요
ch'ŏnshik-i issŏyo

I have a heart condition
심장 질환이 있어요
shimjang chilhwan-i issŏyo

I've been on antibiotics for a week and I'm not getting any better
일주일동안 항생제를 먹었지만 낫지 않아요
iljuil-tongan hangsaengje-rŭl mŏgŏtchiman natchi anayo

it itches
가려워요
karyŏwoyo

I'm on the pill
피임약을 먹고 있어요
p'i-imyak-ŭl mŏkko issŏyo

I'm ... months pregnant
임신 ….개월이에요
imshin … kaewol-ieyo

I'm allergic to penicillin
페니실린에 알레르기가 있어요
p'enisillin-e allerŭgi-ga issŏyo

I've twisted my ankle
발목을 삐었어요
palmok-ŭl ppiŏssŏyo

I fell and hurt my back
넘어져서 허리를 다쳤어요
nŏmŏjyŏsŏ hŏri-rŭl tach'yŏssŏyo

I've had a blackout
기절했어요
kijŏlhaessŏyo

I've lost a filling
봉이 빠졌어요
pong-i ppajyŏssŏyo

is it serious?
심각해요?
shimgak'aeyo?

is it contagious?
전염돼요?
chŏnyŏmdwaeyo?

how is he/she?
어때요?
ŏttaeyo?

how much do I owe you?
얼마에요?
ŏlmaeyo?

can I have a receipt (so I can get the money refunded)?
(환불 받게) 영수증 주시겠어요?
(hwanbul pakke) yŏngsujŭng chushigessŏyo?

Understanding

대기실에 앉아서 기다리세요
taegishil-e anjasŏ kidariseyo
take a seat in the waiting room

어디가 아프세요?
ŏdi-ga ap'ŭseyo?
where does it hurt?

숨을 크게 쉬세요
sum-ŭl k'ŭge shwiseyo
take a deep breath

누우세요
nu-useyo
lie down, please

여기 누르면 아프세요?
yŏgi nurŭmyŏn ap'ŭseyo?
does it hurt when I press here?

… 예방 접종 하셨어요?
… yebang chŏpchong hashyŏssŏyo?
have you been vaccinated against …?

… 에 알레르기 있으세요?
… e allerŭgi issŭseyo?
are you allergic to …?

무슨 약 드시는 거 있으세요?
musŭn yak tŭshinŭn kŏ issŭseyo?
are you taking any other medication?

처방전을 써 드릴게요
ch'ŏbangjŏn-ŭl ssŏ tŭrilgeyo
I'm going to write you a prescription

며칠 안에 좋아질 거에요
myŏch'il an-e choajil kŏ-eyo
it should clear up in a few days

곧 좋아질 거에요
kot choajil kŏ-eyo
it should heal quickly

수술하셔야겠어요
susul-hasyŏyagessŏyo
you're going to need an operation

일주일 후에 다시 오세요
iljuil hu-e tashi oseyo
come back and see me in a week

AT THE CHEMIST'S

Expressing yourself

I'd like some plasters, please
반창고 주세요
panch'anggo chuseyo

I need something for an insect bite/a cough/a bad cold
벌레 물린 데/기침/독감 있는데, 약 좀 주세요
pŏlle mullin te/kich'im/toggam issnŭnte, yak chom chuseyo

I'm allergic to aspirin
아스피린에 알레르기가 있어요
asŭp'irin-e allerŭgi-ga issŏyo

I'd like a bottle of solution for soft contact lenses
소프트 콘택트 렌즈 보존액 주세요
sopŭt'ŭ k'ontaekt'ŭ renjŭ pojonaek chuseyo

Understanding

발라요 *pallayo*	apply
처방전이 필요해요 *ch'ŏbangjŏn-i p'iryohaeyo*	available on prescription only
캡슐 *kaepshyul*	capsule
금기 *kumgi*	contra-indications
크림 *k'ŭrim*	cream
연고 *yŏngo*	ointment
부작용 *pujagyong*	possible side effects
가루약 *karuyak*	powder
좌약 *chwayak*	suppositories
물약 *mullyak*	syrup
알약 *allyak*	tablet

하루 세 번 식전에 드세요
haru se pŏn shikchŏn-e tuseyo

take three times a day before meals

Some informal expressions

침대에서 꼼짝 못 해요 *ch'imdae-esŏ kkomtchak mot haeyo*
to be stuck in bed

아파서 죽겠어요 *ap'asŏ chuggessŏyo* to be as sick as a dog
지독한 감기에 걸렸어요 *chidok'an kamgi-e kŏllyŏssŏyo* to have a
stinking cold

HEALTH

PROBLEMS AND EMERGENCIES

In South Korea, dial 112 for the police and 119 for the fire brigade or an ambulance. However, note that these numbers do not always have English-speaking staff.

Should you require English-speaking assistance in a medical emergency, Asia Emergency Assistance in Seoul provides a 24-hour service liaison between English speakers and Korean hospitals. The number is (02) 790-7561. Note that a fee may be charged for such services.

In an emergency in North Korea, your first point of contact will probably be your tour guide or hotel staff. Note that North Korea may have shortages of basic Western medicines.

The basics

accident	사고 *sago*
ambulance	구급차 *kugŭpch'a*
broken	골절 *koljŏl*
coastguard	해안경비대 *haeangyŏngbidae*
disabled	장애인 *changaein*
doctor	의사 *uisa*
emergency	긴급 상황 *kinggŭp sanghwang*
fire	화재 *hwajae*
fire brigade	소방대 *sobangdae*
hospital	병원 *pyŏngwon*
ill	아파요 *ap'ayo*
injured	부상 *pusang*
late	늦어요 *nŭjŏyo*
police	경찰 *kyŏngch'al*

Expressing yourself

can you help me?
도와주세요
towa-chuseyo

help!
도와주세요!
towa-chuseyo!

fire!
불이야!
pul-iya!

be careful!
조심하세요!
choshimhaseyo!

it's an emergency!
긴급 상황이에요!
kingŭp sanghwang-ieyo!

there's been an accident
사고가 있었어요
sago-ga issŏssŏyo

could I borrow your phone, please?
전화 좀 빌려 주세요
chŏnhwa chom pillyŏ chuseyo

does anyone here speak English?
여기 누가 영어 하세요?
yŏgi nuga yŏngŏ haseyo?

I need to contact the British consulate
영국 대사관에 연락해 주세요
yŏngguk taesagwan-e yŏllak'ae chuseyo

where's the nearest police station?
제일 가까운 경찰서가 어디에요?
cheil kakkaun kyŏngch'alsŏ-ga ŏdi-eyo?

what should I do?
어떻게 해야 돼요?
ŏttŏk'e haeya twaeyo?

my passport/credit card has been stolen
누가 제 여권을/신용카드를 훔쳐 갔어요
nuga che yŏgwŏn-ŭl/shinyong-k'adŭ-rŭl humch'yŏ kassŏyo

my bag's been snatched
가방을 소매치기 당했어요
kabang-ŭl somaech'igi tanghaessŏyo

I've lost ...
… 잃어버렸어요
... ilŏbŏryŏssŏyo

I've been attacked
습격 당했어요
sŭpkyŏk tanghaessŏyo

my son/daughter is missing
아들/딸이 없어졌어요
adŭl/ttal-i ŏpsŏjyŏssŏyo

my car's been towed away
자동차가 견인 당했어요
chadongch'a-ga kyŏnin tanghaessŏyo

I've broken down
자동차가 고장 났어요
chadongch'a-ga kojang nassŏyo

my car's been broken into
누가 제 자동차 안으로 들어왔어요
nuga che chadongch'a an-uro tŭrŏwassŏyo

there's a man following me
어떤 사람이 미행하고 있어요
ŏttŏn saram-i mihaenghago issŏyo

is there disabled access?
장애자용 출입구 있어요?
changaejayong ch'ulipku issŏyo?

can you keep an eye on my things for a minute?
잠깐 제 짐 좀 봐 주시겠어요?
chamkkan che chim chom pa chushigessŏyo?

he's drowning, get help!
사람이 물에 빠졌어요. 도와주세요
saram-i mul-e ppajyŏssŏyo. towa-chuseyo

Understanding

개조심 *kae-joshim*	beware of the dog
고장 수리 *kojang suri*	breakdown service
비상구 *pisanggu*	emergency exit
분실물 *punshilmul*	lost property
산악 구조대 *sanak kujodae*	mountain rescue
고장 *kojang*	out of order

POLICE

Expressing yourself

I want to report something stolen

도난품을 신고하고 싶어요
tonanp'um-ŭl shingohago ship'ŏyo

I need a document from the police for my insurance company

보험 청구를 위해서 경찰 증명서가 필요해요
pohŏm ch'ŏnggu-rŭl wihaesŏ kyŏngch'al chŭngmyŏngsŏ-ga p'ilyohaeyo

Understanding

Filling in forms

성 *sŏng*	surname
이름 *irŭm*	first name
주소 *chuso*	address
우편번호 *up'yŏnbŏnho*	postcode
국가 *kukka*	country
국적 *kukchŏk*	nationality
생년월일 *saengnyŏnwolil*	date of birth
출생지 *ch'ulsaengji*	place of birth
나이 *nai*	age
성별 *sŏngbyŏl*	sex
체류기간 *ch'eryugigan*	duration of stay
도착/출발일 *toch'ak/ch'ulbal-il*	arrival/departure date
직업 *chigŏp*	occupation
여권번호 *yŏgwonbŏnho*	passport number

이 물품은 관세가 있습니다
i mulp'um-ŭn kwanse-ga issŭmnida
there's customs duty to pay on this item

가방 좀 열어 주세요
kabang chom yŏrŏ chuseyo
would you open this bag, please?

뭐가 없습니까?
mŏ-ga ŏpssŭmnikka?
what's missing?

언제 생긴 일입니까?
ŏnje saengin il-imnikka?
when did this happen?

숙박지 어디입니까?
sukpakchi ŏdi-imnikka?
where are you staying?

어떻게 생긴 사람/물건어에요?
ŏttŏk'e saenggin saram/mulgŏn-ieyo?
can you describe him/her/it?

이 서류 좀 작성해 주세요
i sŏryu chom chaksŏnghae chuseyo
would you fill in this form, please?

여기 사인 좀 해 주세요
yŏgi sain chom hae chuseyo
would you sign here, please?

Some informal expressions

쓰리 했어요 *ssŭri haessŏyo* I nicked something
쓰리 당했어요 *ssŭri tanghaessŏyo* I had something nicked
짭새 떴어요 *tchapsae ttŏssŏyo* the cops are coming!

TIME AND DATE

Korea uses both the Gregorian (or Western) calendar (양력 *yangnyŏk*) as well as a lunar calendar (음력 *ŭmnyŏk*) identical to that used in China. The former has become standard in everyday life. However, the latter still determines the dates of several holidays and festivals. In addition, some Koreans use the lunar calendar to express their birthdays.

On a related issue, the way that Koreans calculate their ages is different to that in the West. Firstly, you are considered to already be one year old when you are born. Also, extra years are added to your age not on your birthday but on 1 January. It may thus come as an unpleasant surprise on your trip to Korea to find out that you have suddenly become one or even two years older!

The basics

after	··· 후(에) ... *hu(-e)*
already	벌써 *pŏlssŏ*
always	항상 *hangsang*
at lunchtime	점심때 *chŏmshim-ttae*
at the beginning/end of	처음에/마지막에 *chŏŭm-e/majimak-e*
at the moment	지금 *chigŭm*
before	··· 전(에) ... *chŏn(-e)*
between ... and ...	··· 하고 ··· 사이(에) ... *-hago ... sai(-e)*
day	일 *il*
during	··· 동안 ... *tongan*
early	일찍 *iltchik*
evening	저녁 *chŏnyŏk*
for a long time	오랫동안 *oraettongan*
from ... to ...	··· 에서 ··· 까지 ... *-esŏ ... -kkaji*
from time to time	가끔 *kakkŭm*
in a little while	조금 있다가 *chogŭm ittaga*
in the evening	저녁에 *chŏnyŏk-e*
in the middle of	··· 도중에 ... *tojung-e*
last	마지막 *majimak*

late	늦은 *nŭjŭn*
midday	정오 *chŏngo*
midnight	자정 *chajŏng*
morning	아침 *ach'im*
month	달 *tal*
never	절대로 *chŏldaero*
next	다음 *taŭm*
night	밤 *pam*
not yet	아직 *ajik*
now	지금 *chigŭm*
occasionally	가끔 *kakkŭm*
often	자주 *chaju*
rarely	드물게 *tŭmulge*
recently	최근에 *ch'wegŭn-e*
since	… 이후로 *… ihuro*
sometimes	가끔 *kakkŭm*
soon	곧 *kot*
still	아직도 *ajik-to*
straightaway	당장 *tangjang*
until	… 까지 *… kkaji*
week	일주일 *iljuil*
weekend	주말 *chumal*
year	년 *nyŏn*

Expressing yourself

see you soon!
또 봐요! *(informal; used between friends or to people younger than you)*
tto pwayo!
또 뵙겠습니다! *(formal; used to elders, superiors and new acquaintances)*
tto pekessŭmnida!

see you later!
나중에 봐요! *(informal)*
najung-e pwayo!
나중에 뵙겠습니다! *(formal)*
najung-e pekessŭmnida!

see you on Monday!
월요일에 봐요! *(informal)*
wolyoil-e pwayo!
월요일에 뵙겠습니다! *(formal)*
wolyoil-e pekessŭmnida!

have a good weekend!
주말 재미있게 보내세요!
chumal chaemi-ikke ponaeseyo!

sorry I'm late
늦어서 죄송합니다
nŭjŏsŏ chwesonghamnida

I haven't been there yet
거기 아직 못 가 봤어요
kŏgi ajik mot ka passŏyo

I haven't had time to ...
··· 시간이 없었어요
... shigan-i ŏpsŏssŏyo

I've got plenty of time
시간 많아요
shigan manayo

I'm in a rush
바빠요
pappayo

hurry up!
빨리요!
ppalliyo!

just a minute, please
잠깐만 기다리세요
chamkkan-man kidariseyo

I had a late night
어제 늦게 잤어요
ije nŭkke chassŏyo

I got up very early
아주 일찍 일어났어요
aju iltchik irŏnassŏyo

I waited ages
아주 오래 기다렸어요
aju orae kidaryŏssŏyo

I have to get up very early tomorrow to catch my plane
내일 비행기 타려면 아주 일찍 일어나야 돼요
naeil pihaenggi t'aryŏmyŏn aju iltchik irŏnaya twaeyo

we only have four days left
사일밖에 안 남았어요
sa-il-ppakk-e an namassŏyo

THE DATE

The basics

... ago	⋯ 전에 ... *-chŏn-e*
at the beginning/end of	⋯ 초에／말에 ... *ch'o-e/mal-e*
in the middle of	⋯ 중순에 ... *chungsun-e*
in two days' time	이틀 후 *it'ŭl hu*
last night	어젯밤 *ŏjetpam*
the day after tomorrow	내일 모레 *naeil more*
the day before yesterday	그저께 *kŭjŏkke*
today	오늘 *onŭl*
tomorrow	내일 *naeil*
tomorrow morning/ afternoon/evening	내일 아침／오후／저녁 *naeil ach'im/ohu/ chŏnyŏk*
yesterday	어제 *ŏje*
yesterday morning/ afternoon/evening	어제 아침／오후／저녁 *ŏje ach'im/ohu/chŏnyŏk*

How to express dates

The date is always written and expressed in the order year (년 *nyŏn*), month (월 *wol*), day (일 il). In written documents, it is quite common for the Korean characters to be replaced by the Chinese 年 (year), 月

(month) and 日 (day). Dates are always expressed using Chinese-based numbers (see Numbers chapter).

8 April 2007	2007년 4월 8일 i-chŏn-ch'il-nyŏn sa-wol p'al-il
on the 12th of July	7월 12일에 ch'il-wol ship-i-il-e
in August 1912	1912년 8월에 chŏn-ku-paek-ship-i-nyŏn p'al-wol-e
I was born in 1975	75년생이에요 ch'il-o-nyŏn-saeng-ieyo*

*Note that this is commonly expressed as ch'il-o (seven-five) rather than ch'il-ship-o (seventy-five).

As you can see, the names of months are simply expressed by adding 월 wol ("month") onto the Chinese-based numbers 1–12:

January	1월 il-wol
February	2월 i-wol
March	3월 sam-wol
April	4월 sa-wol
May	5월 o-wol
June	6월 yu-wol
July	7월 ch'il-wol
August	8월 p'al-wol
September	9월 gu-wol
October	10월 shi-wol
November	11월 ship-il-wol
December	12월 ship-i-wol

Note that the expressions for June and October are slightly irregular – the final consonant is dropped from the words for six (originally 육 yuk) and ten (originally 십 ship).

Days of the week

Monday	월요일 wolyoil
Tuesday	화요일 hwayoil
Wednesday	수요일 suyoil
Thursday	목요일 mokyoil

Friday	금요일 *kǔmyoil*
Saturday	토요일 *t'oyoil*
Sunday	일요일 *ilyoil*

Expressing yourself

I came here a few years ago
몇 년 전에 왔어요
myǒt nyǒn chǒn-e wassǒyo

I spent a month here last summer
작년 여름에 한달 동안 있었어요
changnyǒn yǒrǔm-e handal tongan issǒssǒyo

I was here last year at the same time
작년에 같은 시기에 여기 있었어요
changnyǒn-e kat'ǔn shigi-e yǒgi issǒssǒyo

what's the date today?
오늘 날짜가 어떻게 되죠?
onǔl naltcha-ga ǒttǒk'e twechyo?

what day is it today?
오늘 무슨 요일이에요?
onǔl musǔn yoil-ieyo?

it's the 1st of May
5월 1일이에요
o-wol il-il-ieyo

I'm staying until Sunday
일요일까지 있을 거에요
ilyoil-kkaji issǔl kǒ-eyo

we're leaving tomorrow
내일 떠나요
naeil ttǒnayo

I already have plans for Tuesday
화요일에 벌써 약속이 있는데요
hwayoil-e pǒlssǒ yaksok-i innǔndeyo

Understanding

한번/두번 *han-pŏn/tu-pŏn*		once/twice
한 시간에/하루에 세 번 *han shigan-e/haru-e se pŏn*		three times an hour/a day
매일 *maeil*		every day
매주 월요일 *maeju wolyoil*		every Monday

19세기 중반에 지어졌어요

ship-ku segi chungban-e chiŏjyŏssŏyo
it was built in the mid-nineteenth century

여름에 아주 바빠져요

yŏrŭm-e aju pappajyŏyo
it gets very busy here in the summer

언제 떠나세요?

ŏnje ttŏnaseyo?
when are you leaving?

얼마 동안 머무르세요?

ŏlma tongan mŏmurŭseyo?
how long are you staying?

How many days?

When you want to say how many days you stayed somewhere etc, you can usually just say the Chinese-based number followed by the word for day (일 *il*). For example, "eight days" would be 팔 일 *p'al il*. However, for smaller numbers, some special words exist which mean "one day", "two days", etc:

one day	하루 *haru*
two days	이틀 *it'ŭl*
three days	사흘 *sahŭl*
four days	나흘 *nahŭl*
five days	닷새 *tassae*

For one and two days, *haru* and *it'ŭl* must always be used. However, *sahŭl*, *nahŭl* and *tassae* are increasingly replaced by the number + *il* pattern in the speech of many native speakers.

THE TIME

The basics

early	일찍 *iltchik*
half an hour	30분 *sam-ship-bun*
half past	반 *pan*
in the afternoon	오후에 *ohu-e*
in the morning	오전에 *ojŏn-e*
late	늦은 *nŭjŭn*
midday	정오 *chŏngo*
midnight	자정 *chajŏng*
on time	정각에 *chŏnggak-e*
quarter of an hour	십오분 *ship-o-bun*
three quarters of an hour	사십오분 *sa-ship-o-bun*

Telling the time

One confusing thing when expressing the time in Korean is that pure Korean numbers are used for hours, but Chinese-based numbers are used for minutes (and seconds)!

The basic pattern for saying the time is thus to add 시 *shi* ("hour") onto the Korean number for the hour and then 분 *bun* ("minute") onto the Chinese number for the minutes: 7:20 is thus written as 7시 20분 and pronounced *ilgop-shi i-ship-bun*.

To give an approximate time, just add 一쯤 *-tchŭm* to the time expression.

about 8 o'clock	8시쯤 *yŏdol-shi-tchŭm*
about 4:30	4시 30분쯤 *ne-shi sam-ship-bun-tchŭm*

Expressing yourself

what time is it?
몇 시에요?
myŏ shi-eyo?

excuse me, have you got the time, please?
실례합니다. 몇 시에요?
shillehamnida. myŏ shi-eyo?

it's exactly three o'clock
정확히 세 시에요
chŏnghwak'i se shi-eyo

it's nearly one o'clock
한 시 되어가요
han shi tweŏ-gayo

it's ten past one
한시 십분이에요
hanshi ship-bun-ieyo

it's a quarter past one
한시 십오분이에요
hanshi ship-o-bun-ieyo

it's a quarter to one
한시 십오분 전이에요
hanshi ship-o-bun chŏn-ieyo

it's twenty past twelve
열두 시 이십분이에요
yŏl-tu shi iship-bun-ieyo

it's twenty to twelve
열 두시 이십 분 전이에요
yŏl tu-shi i-ship bun chŏn-ieyo

it's half past one
한시 반이에요
han-shi pan-ieyo

I arrived at about two o'clock
두 시쯤 도착했어요
tu shi-tchŭm toch'ak'aessŏyo

I set my alarm for nine
알람시계를 아홉 시에 맞췄어요
allam-shige-rŭl ahop shi-e mach'wossŏyo

I waited twenty minutes
이십 분 동안 기다렸어요
i-ship pun tongan kidaryŏssŏyo

the train was fifteen minutes late
기차가 십오 분 늦었어요
kich'a-ga ship-o bun nŭjŏssŏyo

I got home an hour ago
한 시간 전에 집에 도착했어요
han shigan chŏn-e chip-e toch'ak'aessŏyo

shall we meet in half an hour?
삼십분 있다 만날까요?
sam-ship-bun itta mannalkkayo?

I'll be back in a quarter of an hour
십오분 있다 돌아올게요
ship-o-bun itta tolaolkkeyo

there's a three-hour time difference between ... and ...
…하고 … 세 시간 시차가 있어요
... hago ... se shigan sich'a-ga issŏyo

Understanding

삼십 분마다 떠나요   departs on the hour and the half-hour
sam-ship bun-mada ttŏnayo

열 시부터 네 시까지 열려 있어요 open from 10am to 4pm
yŏl shi-put'ŏ ne shi-kkaji yŏllyŏ issŏyo

매일 저녁 일곱시에 해요
maeil chŏnyŏk ilgop-shi-e haeyo
it's on every evening at seven

삼십 분쯤 걸려요
sam-ship bun-tchŭm kŏllyŏyo
it lasts around an hour and a half

아침 열시에 문 열어요
ach'im yŏl-shi-e mun yŏrŏyo
it opens at ten in the morning

The Korean number system is rather complex. There are two sets of numbers – pure Korean numbers and Chinese-based numbers and also a system of counters.

Pure Korean numbers

The primary use of pure Korean numbers is to count tangible, physical objects such as potatoes, cars, people, tickets and cups of tea. Korean numbers only go up to ninety-nine, so for quantities of 100 onwards the Chinese-based numbers have to be used instead. Even when the quantity is under 100, Chinese-based numbers may be used for quantities over 20 and are almost always used for quantities over 40.

Pure Korean numbers are also used to count hours and age. When giving your age, pure Korean numbers are never replaced by Chinese-based numbers.

Chinese-based numbers

Chinese-based numbers are used in figures, sums and – most importantly – prices. They are also used in place of pure Korean numbers when counting objects in all quantities over 100 and most over 40.

Note that Korean has separate words for ten thousand (만 *man*) and for one hundred million (억 *ŏk*), but no word for million. In Korean, one million is expressed as 백만 *paek-man* "one hundred ten thousands".

Counters

When counting objects, numbers are not used on their own, but followed by a "counter". The concept is not difficult – English also has counters such as "loaves" (of bread), "bars" of chocolate and "pieces" of cake. The difference is that Korean has many more of these counters and they are used all the time! Note that – as shown below – the form of the number that comes before the counter is sometimes slightly different from the original form.

The most common counter is 개 *gae*, which means something like "piece" and can be used with most objects. For example, "three apples" in Korean is 사과 세 개 *sakwa se gae* ("apple three piece"). If you are unsure of the right counter to use, just use 개 *gae* and you will normally be understood, except if you are counting people or animals. Numbers are listed separately and with 개 *gae* in the text below.

Korean numbers

Used for counting objects when quantity is under 40 and for giving your age.

Numbers	Number + *gae* (counter for objects)
1 하나 *hana* (when used alone)	
한 *han* (before a counter)	한 개 *han gae*
2 둘 *tul* (when used alone)	
두 *tu* (before a counter)	두 개 *tu gae*
3 셋 *set* (when used alone)	
세 *se* (before a counter)	세 개 *se gae*
4 넷 *net* (when used alone)	
네 *ne* (before a counter)	네 개 *ne gae*
5 다섯 *tasŏt*	다섯 개 *tasŏt gae*
6 여섯 *yŏsŏt*	여섯 개 *yŏsŏt gae*
7 일곱 *ilgop*	일곱 개 *ilgop gae*
8 여덟 *yŏdol*	여덟 개 *yŏdol gae*
9 아홉 *ahop*	아홉 개 *ahop gae*
10 열 *yŏl*	열 개 *yŏl gae*
11 열 하나 *yŏl hana* (when used alone)	
열 한 *yŏl han* (before a counter)	열 한 개 *yŏl han gae*
12 열 둘 *yŏl tul* (when used alone)	
열 두 *yŏl tu* (before a counter)	열 두 개 *yŏl tu gae*
13 열 셋 *yŏl set* (when used alone)	
열 세 *yŏl se* (before a counter)	열 세 개 *yŏl se gae*
14 열 넷 *yŏl net* (when used alone)	
열 네 *yŏl ne* (before a counter)	열 네 개 *yŏl ne gae*
15 열 다섯 *yŏl tasŏt*	열 다섯 개 *yŏl tasŏt gae*
16 열 여섯 *yŏl yŏsŏt*	열 여섯 개 *yŏl yŏsŏt gae*
17 열 일곱 *yŏl ilgop*	열 일곱 개 *yŏl ilgop gae*

18 열 여덟 *yŏl yŏdol*	열 여덟 개 *yŏl yŏdol gae*
19 열 아홉 *yŏl ahop*	열 아홉 개 *yŏl ahop gae*
20 스물 *sŭmul*	스무 개 *sŭmul gae*
30 서른 *sŏrŭn*	서른 개 *sŏrŭn gae*
40 마흔 *mahŭn*	마흔 개 *mahŭn gae*

(the following are only commonly used for talking about age)

50 쉰 *swhwin*
60 예순 *yesun*
70 일흔 *ilhŭn*
80 여든 *yŏdŭn*
90 아흔 *ahŭn*

Chinese-based numbers

Used for expressing figures, sums and prices and for counting objects when the quantity is over 40.

0 영 *yŏng*	1,500 천오백 *ch'ŏn-o-paek*
공 *kong*	2,000 이천 *i-ch'ŏn*
1 일 *il*	3,000 삼천 *sam-ch'ŏn*
2 이 *i*	5,000 오천 *o-ch'ŏn*
3 삼 *sam*	10,000 만 *man*
4 사 *sa*	11,000 만천 *man-ch'ŏn*
5 오 *o*	12,000 만이천 *man-i-ch'ŏn*
6 육 *yuk*	15,000 만오천 *man-o-ch'ŏn*
7 칠 *ch'il*	20,000 이만 *i-man*
8 팔 *p'al*	30,000 삼만 *sam-man*
9 구 *ku*	50,000 오만 *o-man*
10 십 *ship*	100,000 십만 *ship-man*
20 이십 *i-ship*	110,000 십일만 *ship-il-man*
30 삼십 *sam-ship*	120,000 십이만 *ship-il-man*
50 오십 *o-ship*	150,000 십오만 *ship-o-man*
100 백 *paek*	1,000,000 백만 *paek-man*
200 이백 *i-paek*	1,500,000 백오십만 *paek-o-*
300 삼백 *sam-paek*	*ship-man*
500 오백 *o-paek*	2,000,000 이백만 *i-paek-man*
1,000 천 *ch'ŏn*	5,000,000 오백만 *o-paek-man*
1,100 천백 *ch'ŏn-paek*	10,000,000 천만 *ch'ŏn-man*
1,200 천이백 *ch'ŏn-i-paek*	100,000,000 억 *ŏk*

141

Common counters

Used with Korean numbers (above) for quantities under 40 and with
Chinese-based numbers (below) for higher quantities.

개 *gae* objects
분 *bun* people (honorific – used politely when talking about other people
  you need to respect)
명 *myŏng* people (plain – used when talking about oneself, peers, non-
  acquaintances)
마리 *mari* animals, including whole chickens and fish at the supermarket
잔 *jan* cups or glasses
장 *jang* paper, tickets
권 *gwon* books
병 *byŏng* bottles
대 *dae* vehicles

Ordinal numbers

Except for "first" which is irregular, these are basically formed by adding 번
째 *bŏntchae* to the Korean numbers.

first 첫번째 *chŏp-bŏntchae*
second 두번째 *tu-bŏntchae*
third 세번째 *se-bŏntchae*
fourth 네번째 *ne-bŏntchae*
fifth 다섯번째 *tasŏt-bŏntchae*
sixth 여섯번째 *yŏsŏt-bŏntchae*
seventh 일곱번째 *ilgop-bŏntchae*
eighth 여덟번째 *yŏdŏl-bŏntchae*
ninth 아홉번째 *ahop-bŏntchae*
tenth 열번째 *yŏl-bŏntchae*
twentieth 스무번째 *sŭmu-bŏntchae*

20 plus 3 equals 23
이십 더하기 삼은 이십삼
i-ship tŏhagi sam-ŭn i-ship-sam

20 minus 3 equals 17
이십 빼기 삼은 십칠
i-ship ppaegi sam-ŭn ship-ch'il

20 multiplied by 4 equals 80
이십 곱하기 사는 팔십
i-ship kophagi sa-nŭn p'alship

20 divided by 4 equals 5
이십 나누기 사는 오
i-ship nanugi sa-nŭn o

DICTIONARY

ENGLISH-KOREAN

A

able: to be able to 가능해요
  kanŭnghaeyo
about *(concerning)* … 에 대해
  서 … *-e taehaesŏ*; *(approximately)*
  대강 *taegang*; **to be about to
  do** … 하려고 해요 … *haryŏgo
  haeyo*
above 위 *wi*
abroad 해외에 *haewi-e*
accept 받아요 *padayo*
access *(entrance)* 입구 *ipgu*
accident 사고 *sago* **36, 125**
accommodation 숙박시설
  sukpakshisŏl
across … 건너서 … *kŏnŏsŏ*
adaptor 어댑터 *ŏdaept'ŏ*
address 주소 *chuso* **22**
admission 입장료 *ipchangnyo*
advance: in advance 미리
  miri
advice 조언 *cho-ŏn*; **to ask
  someone's advice**
  조언을 구해요 *cho-ŏn-ŭl
  kuhaeyo*
advise 조언해요 *cho-ŏn-haeyo*
aeroplane 비행기 *pihaenggi*
after … 후에 … *hu-e*
afternoon 오후 *ohu*
again 다시 *tashi*
against … 에 대항하여 … *-e
  taehanghayŏ*
age 나이 *nai*

air 공기 *konggi*; **air conditioning**
  에어컨 *eŏk'ŏn*
airline 항공사 *hanggongsa*
airmail 항공우편 *hanggong-up'yŏn*
airport 공 항 *konghang*
alarm clock 자명종 *chamyŏngjong*,
  알람 시계 *allam-shige*
alcohol 술 *sul*
alive 살아 있어요 *sara issŏyo*
all 전부 *chŏnbu*, 다 *ta*; **all day** 하
  루 종일 *haru chongil*; **all week**
  일주일 내내 *iljuil naenae*; **all
  the time** 항상 *hangsang*, 언제나
  ŏnjena; **all inclusive** 전부 포함
  chŏnbu poham
allergic 알레르기 *allerŭgi* **52, 120,
  122**
almost 거의 *kŏŭi*
already 벌써 *pŏlssŏ*
also … 도 … *tto*
always 항상 *hangsang*, 언제나
  ŏnjena
ambulance 구급차 *kugŭpch'a*
  118
America 미국 *miguk*
American *(n)* 미국사람 *miguk
  saram*; *(adj)* 미국 *miguk*
among … 중에 … *chung-e*
anaesthetic 마취 *mach'wi*
and *(connecting sentences)* 그리고
  kŭrigo; *(connecting nouns)* … 하
  고 … *hago*
animal 동물 *tongmul*
ankle 발목 *palmok*

anniversary 기념일 kinyŏmil

another 다른 tarŭn

answer (n) 대답 taedap

answer (v) 대답해요 taedap'aeyo

answering machine 자동응답기 chadongŭngdapki

ant 개미 kaemi

antibiotics 항생제 hangsaengje

anybody, anyone 아무나 amuna, 아무도 amudo

anything 아무거나 amugŏna, 아무 것도 amugŏt-to

anyway 어쨌든 ŏtchaet-tŭn

appendicitis 맹장 maengjang

appointment 약속 yaksok, 예약 yaeyak **118**; **to make an appointment** 약속해요 yaksok'-aeyo **118**; **to have an appointment (with)** … 하고 약속 있어요 … hago yaksok issŏyo

April 4월 sa-wol

area 지역 chiyŏk; **in the area** 지역에 chiyŏk-e

arm 팔 p'al

around (nearby) 근처에 kŭnch'ŏ-e; (approximately) 대강 taegang

arrange 준비해요 chumbi-haeyo; **to arrange to meet** 만날 약속을 해요 mannal yaksok-ŭl haeyo

arrival 도착 toch'ak

arrive 도착해요 toch'ak'aeyo

art 예술 yesul

artist 예술가 yesulga

as: as soon as possible 가능한 한 빨리 kanŭng-han-han ppalli; **as well as** … 도 … to

ashtray 재떨이 chaettŏri

ask 물어 봐요 murŏ payo; **to ask a question** 질문해요 chilmun-haeyo

aspirin 아스피린 asŭp'irin

asthma 천식 ch'ŏnshik

at … 에 …-e

attack (v) 공격해요 konggyŏk'aeyo **126**

August 8월 p'al-wol

autumn 가을 kaŭl

available 있어요 issŏyo, 이용 가능 해요 iyong kanŭnghaeyo

away 멀리 mŏlli; **10 km away** 십 키로미터 멀리 ship k'iromit'ŏ mŏlli

B

baby 아기 agi; **baby's bottle** 우유병 uyubyŏng, 젖병 chŏppyŏng

back (rear) 뒤 twi; (of body) 허리 hŏri; **at the back of** … 뒤에 … twi-e

backpack 배낭 paenang

bad 나빠요 nappayo; **it's not bad** 나쁘지 않아요 nappŭji anayo

bag 가방 kabang **91**

baggage 짐 chim, 수하물 suhamul

bake 구워요 kuwoyo

baker's 빵집 ppangjip, 제과점 chegwajŏm

balcony 발코니 palk'oni

bandage 붕대 pungdae

bank 은행 ŭnhaeng **103**

banknote 지폐 chip'e

bar 바 pa, 술집 suljip

barbecue 바베큐 *pabek'yu*
bath 욕조 *yokcho*; **to have a bath** 목욕해요 *mogyok'aeyo*; **bath towel** 목욕 수건 *mogyok sukkŏn*
bathroom 화장실 *hwajangshil*
battery 건전지 *kŏnjŏnji*, 바테리 *pat'eri* **36**
be ⋯이에요 *⋯-ieyo*
beach 해변 *haebyŏn*; **beach umbrella** 파라솔 *p'arasol*
beard 수염 *suyŏm*
beautiful 아름다워요 *arŭmdawoyo*
because *(when answering question beginning "why?")* 왜냐하면 *waenyahamyŏn*; *(when providing a reason)* ⋯ 때문이에요 ⋯ *ttaemun-ieyo*; **because of** ⋯ 때문에 ⋯ *ttamun-e*
bed 침대 *ch'imdae*
bee 벌 *pŏl*
before ⋯ 전에 ⋯ *-chŏn-e*
begin 시작해요 *shijak'aeyo*
beginner 초보자 *ch'oboja*
beginning 처음 *ch'ŏŭm*; **at the beginning** 처음에 *ch'ŏŭm-e*
behind 뒤 *twi*
believe 믿어요 *midŏyo*
below 아래 *arae*
beside 옆 *yŏp*
best 제일 좋아요 *cheil choayo*; **the best** 제일 좋은 거 *cheil cho-ŭn kŏ*
better 더 좋아요 *tŏ choayo*; **to get better** 좋아져요 *choajyŏyo*; **it's better to ...** ⋯ 하는 게 좋아요 ⋯ *hanŭn ke choayo*
between 사이 *sai*
bicycle 자전거 *chajŏngŏ*; **bicycle pump** 공기 주입기 *konggi chuipki*

big 큰 *k'ŭn*
bike 자전거 *chajŏngŏ*
bill 계산서 *kesansŏ* **55**
bin 쓰레기통 *ssŭregi-t'ong*
binoculars 망원경 *mangwonggyŏng*
birthday 생일 *saengil*
bit 조금 *chogŭm*
bite *(n)* 물린 상처 *mullin sangch'ŏ*
bite *(v)* 물어요 *murŏyo*
black 검은색 *kŏmŭn-saek*
blanket 담요 *tamyo*
bleed 피를 흘려요 *p'i-rŭl hŭllyŏyo*
blind *(n)* 블라인드 *pŭllaintŭ*; *(adj)* 장님 *changnim*
blister 물집 *muljip*
blood 피 *p'i*, 혈액 *hyŏraek*; **blood pressure** 혈압 *hyŏrap*
blue 파란색 *paransaek*
board *(v) (plane, train, etc)* 탑승해요 *t'apsŭnghaeyo* **30**
boarding 탑승 *t'apsŭng*
boat 배 *pae*, 선박 *sŏmbak*
body 몸 *mom*
book *(n)* 책 *ch'aek*; **book of tickets** 회수권 *hwesugwon*
book *(v)* 예약해요 *yeyak'aeyo*
bookshop 책방 *ch'aekpang*, 서점 *sŏjŏm*
boot *(footwear)* 부츠 *puch'ŭ*; *(of car)* 트렁크 *t'ŭrŏnk'ŭ*
borrow 지루해요 *chiruhaeyo*, 재미없어요 *chaemi-ŏpsŏyo*
botanical garden 식물원 *shingmulwon*
both 둘 다 *tul ta*; **both of us** 우리 둘 다 *uri tul ta*
bottle 병 *pyŏng*; **bottle opener** 병 따개 *pyŏngttagae*
bottom 밑 *mit*, 바닥 *padak*; **at the**

bottom 최저 ch'wejŏ; **at the bottom of** … 밑에 … mit'-e

bowl 사발 sabal, 그릇 kŭrŭt

bra 브래지어 pŭraejiŏ

brake (n) 브레이크 pŭreik'ŭ

brake (v) 브레이크를 밟아요 pŭreik'ŭ-rŭl palbayo

bread 빵 ppang

break (object) 부숴요 pushŏyo; (bone) 부러져요 purŏjyŏyo; **to break one's leg** 다리가 부러져요 tari-ga purŏjyŏyo

break down 고장나요 kojang-nayo **36, 126**

breakdown 고장 kojang; **breakdown service** 고장 수리 kojang suri

breakfast 아침 ach'im **43, 44**; **to have breakfast** 아침을 먹어요 ach'im-ŭl mŏgŏyo

bridge 다리 tari

bring (object) 가지고 와요 kajigo wayo; (people) 데리고 와요 terigo wayo

brochure 팜플렛 p'amp'ŭlet

broken (object) 부서져요 pusŏjyŏyo; (bone) 부러져요 purŏjyŏyo

bronchitis 기관지염 kigwanjiyŏm

brother (elder brother of female) 오빠 oppa; (elder brother of male) 형 hyŏng; (younger brother) 남동생 nam-dongsaeng

brown 갈색 kalsaek

brush 솔 sol, 브러쉬 pŭrŏshi

build 세워요 sewoyo

building 건물 kŏmmul, 빌딩 pilding

bump (v) 부딪쳐요 pudich'yŏyo

bumper 범퍼 pŏmp'ŏ

buoy 구명부이 kumyŏngbui

burn (n) 화상 hwasang

burn: (v) **to burn oneself** 데었어요 teŏssŏyo; **to burn one's finger** 손가락을 데었어요 songarak-ŭl teŏssŏyo

burst (v) 터져요 t'ojyŏyo

bus 버스 pŏsŭ **33, 34**; **bus route** 버스 노선 pŏsŭ nosŏn; **bus station** 버스 터미날 pŏsŭ t'ŏminal; **bus stop** 버스 정류장 pŏsŭ chŏngnyujang

business: business card 출장 ch'uljang; **business trip** 바빠요 pappayo

busy 명함 myŏngham

but 그러나 kŭrŏna

butcher's 정육점 chongyukchŏm

buy 사요 sayo **90, 93**

by … 로 …-ro; **by car** 자동차로 chadongch'a-ro

bye! (said by person leaving to person staying) 안녕히 계세요 annyŏngi keseyo; (said by person leaving to person leaving or by both persons when both are on the move) 안녕히 가세요 annyŏngi kaseyo

C

café 카페 k'ap'e, 다방 tabang

call (n) 전화 chŏnhwa

call (v) 불러요 pullŏyo, 전화해요 chŏnhwahaeyo

call back 다시 전화해요 tashi chŏnhwahaeyo **113**

camera 카메라 k'amera, 사진기 sajingi

camper 캠핑하는 사람

k'aemp'ing-hanŭn saram

camping 캠핑 k'aemp'ing; **to go camping** 캠핑 가요 k'aemp'ing kayo; **camping stove** 캠핑용 난로 k'aemp'ing-yong nallo

campsite 캠핑장 k'aemp'ing-jang **46**

can (n) 캔 k'aen; **can opener** 캔 오프너 k'aen op'ŭnŏ

can (v) 할 수 있어요 hal su issŏyo; **I can't** 할 수 없어요 hal su ŏpsŏyo, 못 해요 mot haeyo

cancel 취소해요 ch'wisohaeyo

candle 촛불 ch'oppul

car 자동차 chadongch'a; **car park** 주차장 chuch'ajang

caravan 캬라반 k'yaraban

card 카드 k'adŭ

carry 가지고 다녀요 kajigo tanyŏyo

case: in case of … … 경우(에) … kyŏngu(-e)

cash 현금 hyŏnggŭm **92**; **to pay cash** 현금으로 내요 hyŏnggŭm-ŭro naeyo

cashpoint 현금 자동 인출기 hyŏnggŭm chadong inch'ulgi **103**

catch 잡아요 chabayo

CD 씨디 ssidi

cemetery (공동)묘지 (kongdong)myoji

centimetre 센티미터 sentimitŏ

centre 중심 chungshim

century 세기 segi

chair 의자 uija

chairlift 리프트 rip'ŭt'ŭ

change (n) 변경 pyŏngyŏng; (money) 잔돈 chanton **92**

change (v) 바꿔요 pakkwoyo, 변경

해요 pyŏngyŏnghaeyo

changing room 탈의실 t'aluishil **95**

channel 채널 ch'aenŏl

chapel 예배당 yebaedang

charge (n) 요금 yogŭm

charge (v) 대금을 청구해요 taegŭm-ŭl chŏngguhaeyo; (battery) 충전해요 ch'ungjŏnhaeyo

cheap 싸요 ssayo

check 확인해요 hwaginhaeyo

check-in 체크인 ch'ek'ŭ-in **30**

check in 체크인 해요 ch'ek'ŭ-in-haeyo

checkout 체크아웃 ch'ek'ŭ-aut

cheers! 건배! kŏmbae!

chemist's 약국 yakkuk

cheque 수표 sup'yo, 계산서 kesansŏ

chest 가슴 kasŭm

child 어린이 ŏrini, 아이 ai

chilly 추워요 ch'uwŏyo

chimney 굴뚝 kulttuk

chin 턱 t'ŏk

China 중국 chungguk

Chinese (n) (person) 중국사람 chungguk saram; (language) 중국어 chungguk-ŏ; (adj) 중국 chungguk

chopsticks 젓가락 chŏkkarak

church 교회 kyohwe; (Catholic) 성당 sŏngdang

cigar 씨가 ssiga

cigarette 담배 tambae

cinema 영화관 yŏnghwagwan

circus 서커스 sŏk'ŏsŭ

city 도시 toshi

clean (adj) 깨끗해요 kkaekkŭt'aeyo

clean (v) 청소해요 ch'ŏngsohaeyo

cliff 절벽 chŏlbyŏk

climate 기후 *kihu*
climbing 등산 *tŭngsan*
cloakroom 휴대품 보관소
  hyudaep'um pogwanso
close (v) 닫아요 *tadayo*, 폐점해요
  p'ejŏmhaeyo
closed 폐점 *p'ejŏm*
closing time 폐점시간 *p'ejŏm-
  shigan*
clothes 옷 *ot*, 의복 *uibok*
clutch 클러치 *k'ŭlŏch'i*
coach (tour coach) 관광버스
  kwanggwang-pŏsŭ; (express coach)
  고속버스 *kosok-pŏsŭ*
coast 해안 *hae-an*
coathanger 옷걸이 *ot-kŏri*
cockroach 바퀴벌레 *pak'wibŏlle*
coffee 커피 *kŏp'i*
coin 동전 *tongjŏn*
Coke® 코카콜라 *k'ok'ak'olla*
cold (n) 감기 *kamgi*; **to have
  a cold** 감기 걸렸어요*kamgi
  kŏllyŏssŏyo*
cold (adj) 추워요 *ch'uwoyo*; **it's
  cold** 날씨가 추워요 *nalssi-
  ga ch'uwoyo*; **I'm cold** 추워요
  ch'uwoyo
collection 콜렉션 *k'ollekshyŏn*
colour 색 *saek*, 색깔 *saekkal*
comb 빗 *pit*
come 와요 *wayo*
come back 돌아와요 *torawayo*
come in 들어와요 *tŭrŏwayo*
come out 나와요 *nawayo*
comfortable 편안해요
  p'yŏnanhaeyo
company 회사 *hwesa*
complain 불평해요 *pulp'yŏnghaeyo*
comprehensive insurance 종합

보험 *chonghap-pohŏm*
computer 컴퓨터 *k'ŏmp'yut'ŏ*
concert 음악회 *ŭmak'we*, 연주회
  yŏnjuhwe; **concert hall** 콘서트홀
  k'onsŏt'ŭ-hol
concession 할인 *harin* **28**
condom 콘돔 *k'ondom*
confirm 확인해요 *hwagin-haeyo* **30**
connection 관계 *kwange*, 접속
  chŏpsok **30**
constipation 변비 *pyŏnbi*
consulate 영사관 *yŏngsagwan* **125**
contact (n) 연락 *yŏllak*; **contact
  lenses** 콘택트 렌즈 *k'ont'aekt'ŭ
  renjŭ*
contact (v) 연락해요 *yŏllak'aeyo*
  111
contagious 전염되요 *chŏnyŏm-
  tweyo*
contraceptive 피임 *p'iim*
cook (v) 요리해요 *yori-haeyo*
cooked 조리된 *choritwen*
cooking 요리 *yori*; **to do the
  cooking** 요리해요 *yori-haeyo*
cool 시원해요 *shiwonhaeyo*
corkscrew 코르크 따개 *k'orŭk'ŭ
  ttagae*
correct 정확해요 *chŏnghwak'aeyo*
cost 비용 *piyong*
cotton 면 *myŏn*; **cotton bud** 면
  봉 *myŏn-bong*; **cotton wool** 탈지
  면 *t'alji-myŏn*
cough (n) 기침 *kich'im*; **to have
  a cough** 기침이 나요 *kich'im-i
  nayo*
cough (v) 기침해요 *kich'im-haeyo*
count 세요 *seyo*
country 나라 *nara*
countryside 시골 *shigol*

course: of course 물론이에요
  mullon-ieyo
cover (n) 덮개 tŏpkae
cover (v) 덮어요 tŏp'ŏyo
credit card 신용카드 shinyong-
  k'adŭ **41, 92**
cross (n) 십자가 shipchari
cross (v) 횡단해요 hwingdanhaeyo
cruise 크루즈 k'ŭrujŭ
cry 울어요 urŏyo
cup 컵 k'ŏp
currency 통화 t'onghwa
customs 세관 segwan
cut 절단해요 chŏldanhaeyo; **to cut
  oneself** 베었어요 peŏssŏyo
cycle path 싸이클 도로 ssaik'ŭl
  toro

D

damaged 망가진 manggajin
damp 눅눅해요 nuknuk'aeyo
dance (n) 춤 ch'um
dance (v) 춤 춰요 ch'um chŏyo
dangerous 위험해요 wihŏmhaeyo
dark (lacking in light) 어두워요
  ŏduwoyo; (colour, shade) 진해
  요 chinhaeyo; **dark blue** 곤색
  konsaek
date (n) 날짜 naltcha; **out of date**
  오래된 oraedwen; **date of birth**
  생년월일 saengnyŏnwolil
daughter 딸 ttal
day 날 nal; **the day after
  tomorrow** 모레 more; **the
  day before yesterday** 그저께
  kŭjŏkke
dead 죽었어요 chugŏssŏyo
deaf 청각장애인 chŏnggak-

changaein
dear (expensive) 비싸요 pissayo
debit card 현금카드 hyŏngŭm-
  k'adŭ
December 12월 ship-i-wol
declare 신고해요 shingohaeyo
deep 깊어요 kip'ŏyo
degree 정도 chŏngdo
delay 연기 yŏngi
delayed 연기되요 yŏngi-tweyo
dentist 치과 ch'igwa
deodorant 방향제 panghyangje
department 과 kwa; **department
  store** 백화점 paek'wajŏm
departure 출발 ch'ulbal
depend 의존해요 uijonhaeyo
deposit 보증금 pojŭnggŭm
dessert 디저트 tijŏtŭ, 후식 hyushik
  53
develop: to get a film developed
  필름을 현상해요 p'illŭm-ŭl
  hyŏnsanghaeyo
diabetes 당뇨병 tangnyobyŏng
dialling code 국번 kukpŏn
diarrhoea: to have diarrhoea 설
  사해요 sŏlsa-haeyo
die 죽어요 chugŏyo
diesel 디젤 tijel
diet 다이어트 taiŏt'ŭ
different (from) ... (하고) 달라요
  ... (hago) tallayo
difficult 어려워요 ŏryŏwoyo
digital camera 디지털 카메라
  tijit'ŏl k'amera
dinner 저녁 chŏnyŏk; **to have
  dinner** 저녁을 먹어요 chŏnyŏk-
  ŭl mŏgŏyo
direct 직접 chikchŏp
direction 방향 panghyang

directory (전화) 번호부 (chŏnhwa) pŏnhobu; **directory enquiries** 번호 안내 pŏnho annae

dirty (adj) 더러워요 tŏrŏwoyo

disabled 장애인 changaein **126**

disaster 재앙 chae-ang

disco 디스코 tisŭk'o

discount 할인 harin **78**; **to give someone a discount** 할인해 줘 요 harin-hae chŏyo; **discount fare** 할인 가격harin kagyŏk

dish 요리 yori; **dish towel** 행주 haengju

dishes 설거지 sŏlgŏji; **to do the dishes** 설거지해요 sŏlgŏji-haeyo

dishwasher 디쉬 워셔 tishi woshyŏ

disinfect 소독해요 sodok'aeyo

disposable 일회용 ilhwayong

disturb 방해해요 panghaehaeyo; **do not disturb** 깨우지 마세요 kkaeuji maseyo

diving: to go diving 다이빙해요 taibing-haeyo

do 해요 haeyo

doctor 의사 uisa **117**

door 문 mun; **door code** 문 비밀 번호 mun pimilbŏnho

downstairs 아래층 araech'ŭng

draught beer 생맥주 saeng-maekchu

dress: to get dressed 옷 입어 요 ot ibŏyo

dressing 드레싱 tŭresing

drink (n) 음료수 umnyosu; **to go for a drink** 한잔하러 가요 han-chan-harŏ kayo **50**; **to have a drink** 한잔해요 han-chan-haeyo

drink (v) 마셔요 mashyŏyo

drinking water 식수 shiksu

drive: (n) **to go for a drive** 드라이 브해요 tŭraibŭ-haeyo

drive (v) 운전해요 unjŏnhaeyo

driving licence 운전면허 unjŏnmyŏnhŏ

drops 안약 anyak

drown 물에 빠져요 mul-e ppajyŏyo

drugs (medicine) 약 yak; (illegal) 마 약 mayak

drunk 술취해요 sulch'wihaeyo

dry (adj) 건조해요 kŏnjohaeyo; **dry cleaner's** 세탁소 set'akso

dry (v) 말려요 mallyŏyo

duck 오리 ori

during … 동안 … tongan; **during the week** 주중에 chujung-e

dustbin 쓰레기통 ssŭregit'ong

E

each 각각의 kakkak-ui; **each person** 각자 kakcha

ear 귀 kwi

early 일찍 iltchik

earplugs 귀마개 kwimagae

earrings 귀걸이 kwigŏri

earth 땅 ttang

east 동 tong; **in the east** 동쪽에 tong-tchok-e; **(to the) east of** … (의) 동쪽 … (-e) tong-tchok

Easter 부활절 puhwaljŏl

easy 쉬워요 shwiwoyo

eat 먹어요 mŏgŏyo **50**

economy class 일반석 ilbansŏk

electric 전기 chŏnggi; **electric shaver** 전기 면도기 chŏnggi myŏndogi

electricity 전기 *chŏnggi*; **electricity meter** 전기 미터 *chŏnggi mit'ŏ*

e-mail 이메일 *imeil*; **e-mail address** 이메일 주소 *imeil chuso* **22, 108**

embassy 대사관 *taesagwan*

emergency 긴급 상황 *kingŭp sanghwang*; **in an emergency** 비상시 *pisangshi*; **emergency exit** 비상구 *pisanggu*

empty 비어 있어요 *piŏ issŏyo*

end 끝 *kkŭt*; **at the end of** … (의) 끝에 … *(-e) kkŭt'-e*; **at the end of the street** 길 끝에 *kil kkŭt-e*

engaged *(in use)* 사용중 *sayongjung*; *(to be married)* 약혼했어요 *yak'onhaessŏyo*

engine 엔진 *enjin*

England 영국 *yŏngguk*, 잉글랜드 *ingŭllaendŭ*

English *(n)* 영어 *yŏngŏ*; *(adj)* 영국 *yŏngguk*

Englishman, Englishwoman 영국 사람 *yŏngguk saram*

enjoy … 즐겨요 … *chulgyŏyo*; **to enjoy oneself** 재미있는 시간 보내요 *chaemi-innŭn shigan ponaeyo*; **enjoy your meal!** 맛있게 드세요 *mashikke tŭseyo*

enough 충분해요 *ch'ungbunhaeyo*

entrance 입구 *ipku*

envelope 봉투 *pongt'u* **106**

epilepsy 간질병 *kanjilbyŏng*

equipment 장비 *changbi*

espresso 에스프레소 *esŭp'ŭreso*

euro 유로 *yuro*

Europe 유럽 *yurŏp*

European *(person)* 유럽 사람 *yurŏp saram*

evening 저녁 *chŏnyŏk*; **in the evening** 저녁에 *chŏnyŏk-e*

every 모든 *modŭn*; **every day** 매 일 *maeil*

everybody, everyone 모든 사람 *modŭn saram*

everywhere 어디든지 *ŏdidŭnji*

except … 제외하고 … *chewehago*

exceptional 예외 *yewe*

excess 초과 *ch'ogwa*

exchange 교환해요 *kyohwanhaeyo*; **exchange rate** 환율 *hwanyul*

excuse *(n)* 변명 *pyŏmmyŏng*

excuse *(v)* 용서해요 *yongsŏhaeyo*; **excuse me** 실례합니다 *sillehamnida*

exhaust 다 써요 *ta ssŏyo*; **exhaust pipe** 배기관 *paegigwan*

exhausted 지쳤어요 *chich'yŏssŏyo*

exhibition 전시회 *chŏnshihwe* **77**

exit 출구 *ch'ulgu*

expensive 비싸요 *pissayo*

expiry date 유효기간 *yuhyo-kigan*

extra 여분 *yŏbun*

eye 눈 *nun*

F

face 얼굴 *ŏlgul*

facecloth 세안용 타올 *se-anyong t'aol*

fact: in fact 사실은 *sashil-ŭn*

faint 기절해요 *kijŏlhaeyo*

fair *(n)* *(trade fair)* 박람회 *pangnamhwe*; *(show)* 공진회 *kongjinhwe*

fall *(v)* 떨어져요 *ttŏlŏjyŏyo*; **to fall**

asleep 잠 들어요 *cham tŭrŏyo*;
to fall ill 병 들어요 *pyŏng tŭrŏyo*

family 가족 *kajok*

fan (*electric*) 선풍기 *sŏnp'unggi*

far 멀어요 *mŏrŏyo*; **far from** …
에서 멀어요 *…-esŏ mŏrŏyo*

fare 요금 *yogŭm*

fast 빨라요 *ppallayo*

fast-food restaurant 패스트 푸
드 식당 *p'aesŭt'ŭ p'udŭ shiktang*

fat 지방 *chibang*

father 아버지 *abŏji*

favour 부탁 *put'ak*; **can you do
me a favour?** 부탁이 있는데요
put'ak-i innŭndeyo

favourite 제일 좋아해요 *cheil
choahaeyo*

fax 팩스 *p'aeksŭ*

February 2월 *i-wol*

fed up 질렸어요 *chillyŏssŏyo*; **to be
fed up (with)** … 에 질렸어요
…-e chillyŏssŏyo

feel 느껴요 *nŭkkyŏyo* **119**; **to feel
good/bad** 기분이 좋아요／나
빠요 *kibun-i choayo/nappayo*

feeling 기분 *kibun*

ferry 페리 *p'eri*

festival 축제 *ch'ukche*

fetch: to go and fetch (*person*)
가서 … 데리고 와요 *kasŏ …
terigo wayo*; (*object*) 가서 … 가지
고 와요 *kasŏ … kajigo wayo*

fever 열 *yŏl*; **to have a fever** 열
이 있어요 *yŏl-i issŏyo*

few 조금 *chogŭm*

fiancé, fiancée 약혼자 *yak'onja*

fight (*v*) 싸워요 *ssawoyo*

fill 가득 채워요 *kadŭk ch'aewoyo*

fill in 기입해요 *kiip'aeyo*

fill up: to fill up with petrol 기름
을 넣어요 *kirŭm-ŭl nŏ-ŏyo*

filling (*in tooth*) 봉 *pong*

film (*for camera*) 필름 *p'illŭm* **99**

finally (*last of all*) 마지막으로
majimak-uro; (*at last*) 드디어
tudiŏ

find 찾아요 *ch'ajayo*

fine (*n*) 벌금 *pŏlgŭm*

fine (*adj*) 좋아요 *choayo*

finger 손가락 *songarak*

finish 끝나요 *kkŭnnayo*

fire 불 *pul*, 화재 *hwajae*; **fire!** 불
이야! *pul-iya!*; **fire brigade** 소방
대 *sobangdae*

fireworks 불꽃놀이 *pulkkonnori*

first 처음 *ch'ŏŭm*; **first (of all)**
먼저 *mŏnjŏ*; **first class** 일등석
ildŭngsŏk; **first floor** 일층 *il-
ch'ŭng*; **first name** 이름 *irŭm*

fish (*n*) 생선 *saengsŏn*

fishmonger's 생선장수
saengsŏnjangsu

fitting room 탈의실 *t'aluishil*

fizzy 탄산 *t'ansan*

flash 플래시 *p'ŭllaeshi*

flask 보온병 *po-ombyŏng*

flat (*adj*) 평평해요
p'yŏngpy'ŏnghaeyo; **flat tyre** 펑크
p'ŏngk'ŭ

flat (*n*) 아파트 *ap'at'ŭ*

flavour 맛 *mat*

flaw 흠 *hŭm*

flight 비행기 편명 *pihaenggi
p'yŏnmyŏng*

flip-flops 슬리퍼 *sŭllip'ŏ*

floor 마루 *maru*; **on the floor** 마
루에 *maru-e*

flu 독감 *tokkam*

fly (n) 파리 p'ari
fly (v) 날아가요 naragayo
food 음식 ŭmshik; **food poisoning**
식중독 shikchungdok
foot 발 pal
for … 동안 … tongan; **for an
hour** 한 시간 동안 han shigan
tongan
forbidden 금지됐어요
kŭmjidwaessŏyo
forecast 예보 yebo
forehead 이마 ima
foreign 외국 weguk
foreigner 외국사람 weguk-saram
forest 숲 sup
fork 포크 p'ok'ŭ
former 이전 ijŏn
forward (adj) 앞의 ap'-e
four-star petrol 포스타 휘발유
p'osŭt'a hwibaryu
fracture 골절 koljŏl
fragile 깨지기 쉬운 kkaejigi swium
free 무료 muryo
freezer 냉동고 naengdonggo
Friday 금요일 kŭmyoil
fridge 냉장고 naengjanggo
fried 튀김 t'wigim
friend 친구 ch'ingu
from … 부터 … put'ŏ; **from …
to …** … 부터 … 까지 … put'ŏ
… kkaji
front 앞 ap; **in front of** 앞에
ap'-e
fry 튀겨요 t'wigyŏyo
frying pan 후라이팬 huraip'aen
full 가득 kadŭk; **full board** 삼식
제공 samshik chegong; **full fare,
full price** 정규 요금 chŏnggyu
yogŭm

funfair 놀이공원 nori-kongwon
fuse 퓨즈 p'yuujŭ

G

gallery 미술관 misulgwan
game 게임 geim
garage (for repairs) 자동차 수리
공장 chadongch'a suri kongjang **36**;
(for parking) 차고 ch'ago
garden 정원 chŏngwon
gas 가스 kasŭ; **gas cylinder** 가스
실린더 kasŭ sillindŏ
gastric flu 위장장애 인플루엔자
wijangjangae inp'ŭlluenja
gate 대문 taemun
gauze 가제 kaje
gay 동성연애자 tongsŏngyŏnaeja
gearbox 기어박스 kiŏbaksŭ
general 일반적 ilbanjŏk
gents' (toilet) 남자용 (화장실)
namja-yong (hwajangshil)
get 받아요 padayo
get off 내려요 naeryŏyo
get up 일어나요 irŏnayo
gift wrap 선물 포장 sŏmmul
p'ojang
girl 여자 yŏja; (younger) 소녀 sonyŏ
girlfriend 여자친구 yŏja-ch'ingu
give 줘요 chŏyo
give back 돌려줘요 tollyŏ-chŏyo
glass 잔 chan; **a glass of water/of
wine** 물／와인 한 잔 mul/wain
han chan
glasses 안경 angyŏng
go 가요 kayo; **to go to Japan** 일
본에 가요 ilbon-e kayo; **we're
going home tomorrow** 내일
집에 가요 naeil chip-e kayo

go in 들어가요 *tŭrŏgayo*
go out 나가요 *nagayo*
go with 어울려요 *ŏullyŏyo*
golf 골프 *kolp'ŭ*; **golf course** 골프
장 *kolp'ŭ-jang*
good 좋아요 *choayo*; **good
morning** 안녕하세요
annyŏnghaseyo; **good afternoon**
안녕하세요 *annyŏnghaseyo*;
good evening 안녕하세요
annyŏnghaseyo
goodbye *(said by person leaving to
person staying)* 안녕히 계세요
annyŏngi keseyo; *(said by person
leaving to person leaving or by both
persons when both are on the move)*
안녕히 가세요 *annyŏngi kaseyo*
goodnight *(when going to bed)*
안녕히 주무세요 *annyŏnghi
chumuseyo*
goods 상품 *sangp'um*
grams 그램 *kŭraem*
grass 잔디 *chandi*
great 훌륭해요 *hullyunghaeyo*
Great Britain 영국 *yŏngguk*
green 녹색 *noksaek*
grey 회색 *hwesaek*
grocer's 채소가게 *ch'aeso-kagae*
ground 지상 *chisang*, 땅 *ttang*; **on
the ground** 지상에 *chisang-e*;
ground floor 일층 *il-ch'ŭng*
grow 자라요 *charayo*
guarantee 보증 *pojŭng*
guest 손님 *sonnim*; **guest house**
여관 *yŏgwan*
guide 안내 *annae* 71
guidebook 안내책자
annaech'aekcha
guided tour 가이드 투어 *kaidŭ*

t'uŏ
gynaecologist 산부인과
sambuingwa

H

hair 머리(카락) *mŏri(k'arak)*
hairdresser 미용실 *miyongshil*
hairdrier 헤어드라이어 *heŏ-
dŭraiŏ*
half 반 *pan*; **half a litre/kilo** 반
리터／킬로 *pan rit'ŏ/k'illo*; **half an
hour** 반 시간 *pan shigan*
half-board 아침 저녁 제공
ach'im chŏnyŏk chegong
hand 손 *son*; **hand luggage** 핸드
캐리 *haendŭ-k'aeri*
handbag 핸드백 *haendŭ-baek*
handbrake 싸이드 브레이크
ssaidŭ pŭreik'ŭ
handicapped 장애 *changae*
handkerchief 손수건 *sonsugŏn*
hand-made 수제품 *sujep'um*
hangover 숙취 *sukch'wi*
happen 발생해요 *palsaenghaeyo*
happy 행복해요 *haengbok'aeyo*
hard *(not easy)* 어려워요 *ŏryŏwoyo*;
(not soft) 딱딱해요 *ttakttak'aeyo*
hat 모자 *moja*
hate 싫어해요 *shirŏhaeyo*
have 있어요 *issŏyo*; **I don't have**
없어요 *ŏpsŏyo*
have to 해야 해요 *haeya haeyo*;
I have to go 가야 해요 *kaya
haeyo*
hay fever 꽃가루 알레르기 *kkot-
karu allerŭgi*
he 그 남자 *kŭ namja*
head 머리 *mŏri*

headache: to have a headache 머리가 아파요 *mŏri-ga ap'ayo*

headlight 전조등 *chŏnjodŭng*

health 건강 *kŏngang*

hear 들어요 *tŭrŏyo*

heart 심장 *shimjang*; **heart attack** 심장마비 *shimjang-mabi*

heat 열 *yŏl*

heating 난방 *nambang*

heavy 무거워요 *mugŏwoyo*

hello 안녕하세요 *annyŏnghaseyo*

helmet 헬멧 *helmet*

help (n) 도움 *toum*; **to call for help** 도움을 요청해요 *toum-ŭl yoch'ŏnghaeyo*; **help!** 도와 주세요! *towa juseyo!*

help (v) 도와 줘요 *towa jŏyo* **125**

her 그 여자(의) *ku yŏja(-e)*

here 여기 *yŏgi*; **here is/are** 여기 ⋯ 있어요 *yŏgi ... issŏyo*

hi! 안녕하세요! *annyŏnghaseyo!*

hi-fi 하이파이 *haip'ai*

high 높아요 *nop'ayo*; **high blood pressure** 고혈압 *ko-hyŏrap*; **high tide** 만조 *manjo*

hiking 등산 *tŭngsan*; **to go hiking** 등산해요 *tŭngsan-haeyo*

hill 언덕 *ŏndŏk*

hill-walking 등산 *tŭngsan*; **to go hill-walking** 등산해요 *tŭngsan-haeyo*

hip (bone) 골반 *kolban*; (buttocks) 엉덩이 *ŏngdŏngi*

hire (n) 임대 *imdae*

hire (v) 빌려요 *pillyŏyo*, 임대해요 *imdae-haeyo*, 그 남자(의) *kŭ namja-(ui)* **36, 82**

hitchhike 히치하이킹해요 *hich'ihaik'ing-haeyo*

hitchhiking 히치하이킹 *hich'ihaik'ing*

hold 잡아요 *chabayo*

hold on! (on the phone) 잠깐 기다리세요! *chamkkan kidariseyo!*

holiday(s) 휴가 *hyuga*; **on holiday** 휴가 중에 *hyuga chung-e*

home 집 *chip*; **at home** 집에 *chip-e*; **to go home** 집에 가요 *chip-e kayo*

homosexual 동성애 *tongsŏngae*

honest 정직해요 *chŏngjik'aeyo*

honeymoon 신혼여행 *shinhonyŏhaeng*

horse 말 *mal*

hospital 병원 *pyŏngwon*

hot 뜨거워요 *ttŭgŏwoyo*; **it's hot** 뜨거워요 *ttŭgŏwoyo*; **hot drink** 뜨거운 음료수 *ttŭgŏun umnyosu*; **hot chocolate** 코코아 *k'ok'oa*

hotel 호텔 *hot'el*

hour 시간 *shigan*; **an hour and a half** 한 시간 반 *han shigan pan*

house 집 *chip*

housework 집안일 *chibanil*; **to do the housework** 집안일을 해요 *chibanil-ŭl haeyo*

how 어떻게 *ŏttŏk'e*; **how are you?** 안녕하세요? *annyŏnghaseyo?*

hungry: to be hungry 배고파요 *paegop'ayo*

hurry: to be in a hurry 급해요 *kŭp'aeyo*

hurry (up) 서둘러요 *sŏdullŏyo*

hurt: it hurts 아파요 *ap'ayo*; **my head hurts** 머리가 아파요 *mŏri-ga ap'ayo* **119**

husband 남편 *namp'yŏn*

I

I (polite) 저 chŏ; (informal) 나 na;
I'm English 저는 영국 사람이
에요 chŏ-nŭn yŏngguk saram-ieyo;
I'm 22 (years old) 저는 스물
두 살이에요 chŏ-nŭn sŭmul-tu
sal-ieyo

ice 얼음 ŏrŭm; **ice cream** 아이스
크림 aisŭk'ŭrim

identity: **identity card** 신분증
shimbunjŭng; **identity papers** 신
분증명서 shimbunjŭngmyŏngsŏ

if 만약 manyak

ill 아파요 ap'ayo

illness 병 pyŏng

important 중요해요 chungyohaeyo

in …에 …-e; **in England/2007/
Korean** 영국에／2007년에／한
국말로 yŏngguk-e/i-ch'ŏn-ch'il-
nyŏn-e/hankkuk-mal-lo; **in the 19th
century** 십구 세기에 ship-ku
segi-e; **in an hour** 한 시간 후에
han shigan hu-e

included 포함 p'oham 55

independent 독립해요
tongnip'aeyo

indicator (on car) 깜박이 kkambagi

infection 감염 kamyŏm

information 정보 jŏngbo 76

injection 주사 chusa

injured 다쳤어요 tach'yŏssŏyo

insect 벌레 pŏlle

insecticide 살충제 salch'ungje

inside 안 an

insomnia 불면증 pulmyŏnjŭng

instant coffee 인스턴트 커피
insŭt'ŏnt'ŭ k'ŏp'i

instead 대신 taeshin; **instead of**
… 대신에 … taeshin-e

insurance 보험 pohŏm 37

intend to … … 하려고 해요 …
haryŏgo haeyo

international 국제 kukche;
**international money
order** 국제송금신청
kukchesonggŭmshinjŏng

Internet 인터넷 int'ŏnet; **Internet
café** (Korean-style) PC방 PC-bang;
(Western-style) 인터넷 카페
int'ŏnet k'ap'e 108

invite 초청해요 ch'och'ŏnghaeyo

Ireland 아일랜드 aillaendŭ

Irishman, Irishwoman 아일랜드
사람 aillaendŭ saram

iron (for clothes) 다리미 tarimi

iron (v) 다리미질 해요 tarimijil
haeyo

island 섬 sŏm

it 그 거 ku kŏ

itchy: **it's itchy** 가려워요
karyŏwoyo

item 품목 p'ummok

J

jacket 자켓 jak'et

January 1월 il-wol

Japan 일본 ilbon

Japanese (n) (person) 일본 사
람 ilbon saram; (language) 일본어
ilbon-ŏ; (adj) 일본 ilbon

jetlag 시차 shich'a

jeweller's 보석상 posŏksang

jewellery 보석 posŏk

job 직업 chigŏp

jogging 조깅 choging

journey 여행 yŏhaeng

jug 물병 *mulbyŏng*
juice 주스 *chusŭ*
July 7월 *ch'il-wol*
jumper 점퍼 *chŏmp'ŏ*
June 6월 *yu-wol*
just: just before 조금 전
chogŭm chŏn; just a little 조금
만 *chogŭm-man*; just one 하나
만 *hana-man*; I've just arrived
금방 도착했어요 *kŭmbang
toch'ak'aessŏyo*; just in case 만약
의 경우에 *manyak-e kyŏngu-e*

K

karaoke parlour 노래방
noraebang
keep 계속 지켜요 *kesok chik'yŏyo*
key 열쇠 *yŏlswe* 36, 41, 44
kidney 신장 *shinjang*
kill 죽여요 *chugyŏyo*
kilometre 킬로미터 *k'illomit'ŏ*
kind: what kind of ...? 무슨 ...?
musŭn ...?
kitchen 친절해요 *ch'injŏlhaeyo*
knee 무릎 *murŭp*
knife 칼 *k'al*
knock down 때려 눕혀요 *ttaeryŏ
nup'yŏyo*
know 알아요 *arayo*; I don't know
몰라요 *mollayo*
Korea 한국 *hanguk*
Korean (n) (person) 한국 사람
hanguk saram; (language) 한국어
hanguk-ŏ; (adj) 한국 *hanguk*

L

ladies' (toilet) 여자용 (화장실)
yŏjayong (hwajangshil)

lake 호수 *hosu*
lamp 램프 *raemp'ŭ*
landmark 경계표 *kyŏnggep'yo*
landscape 경치 *kyŏngch'i*
language 언어 *ŏnŏ*
laptop 노트북 *not'ŭbuk*
last (adj) 지난 *chinan*; last year 작
년 *changnyŏn*
last (v) 계속돼요 *kesoktwaeyo*
late 늦어요 *nŭjŏyo*
late-night opening 심야영업
shimyayŏngŏp
laugh 웃음 *usŭm*
launderette 세탁소 *set'akso*
lawyer 변호사 *pyŏnhosa*
leaflet 안내장 *annaejang*
leak (n) 누수 *nusu*
learn 배워요 *paewoyo*
least: the least 최소 *ch'weso*; at
least 적어도 *chŏkŏ-do*
leave 떠나요 *ttŏnayo*
left 왼쪽 *wentchok*; to the left
(of) ... (의) 왼쪽에 ...(-e)
wentchok-e
left-luggage (office) 수하물 보관
소 *suhamul pogwanso*
leg 다리 *tari*
lend 빌려 줘요 *pillyŏ chŏyo*
lens 렌즈 *renjŭ*
less 적어요 *chŏgŏyo*; less than ...
보다 적어요 *... poda chŏgŏyo*
let 임대해요 *imdaehaeyo*
letter 편지 *p'yŏnji*
letterbox 편지함 *p'yŏnjiham*
library 도서관 *tosŏgwan*
life 인생 *insaeng*, 생명 *saengmyŏng*
lift 엘리베이터 *ellibeit'ŏ*, 승강기
sŭngganggi 44
light (adj) (not dark) 밝아요 *palgayo*;

(not heavy) 가벼워요 *kabyŏwoyo*;
light blue 밝은 청색 *palgŭn
ch'ŏngsaek*
light (n) (electric) 불 *pul*; **do you
have a light?** 라이터 있어
요? *rait'ŏ issŏyo?*; **light bulb** 전
구 *chŏngu*
light (v) 불을 붙여요 *pul-ŭl
puch'yŏyo*
lighter 라이터 *rait'ŏ*
lighthouse 등대 *tŭngdae*
like (adv) 처럼 *...-ch'ŏrŏm*
like (v) 좋아해요 *choahaeyo*; **I'd
like ...** ... 주세요 *... chuseyo*
line 줄 *chul* **34**
lip 입술 *ipsul*
listen 들어요 *tŭrŏyo*
listings magazine 정보지
chŏngboji
litre 리터 *rit'ŏ*
little (adj) 적어요 *chŏgŏyo*
little (adv) 적게 *chŏkke*
live 살아요 *sarayo*
liver 간 *kan*
living room 거실 *kŏshil*
local time 현지시간 *hyŏnji-shigan*
lock (v) 잠가요 *chamgayo*
long 길어요 *kirŏyo*; **a long time**
오래 *orae*; **how long ...?** 얼마
동안 ...? *ŏlma-tongan ...?*
look: to look at ... 봐요 *... payo*;
to look tired 피곤해 보여요
p'igonhae poyŏyo
look after 보살펴 줘요 *posalp'yŏ
chŏyo*
look for 찾아요 *ch'ajayo* **16**
look like 비슷해 보여요 *pisŭt'ae
poyŏyo*
lorry 트럭 *t'ŭrŏk*

lose 잃어요 *irŏyo* **36**; **to get lost**
길을 잃었어요 *kil-ŭl irŏssŏyo* **16**
lot: a lot (of) 많이 *mani*
loud 크게 *k'ŭge*
low 낮아요 *najayo*; **low blood
pressure** 저혈압 *chŏhyŏrap*; **low
tide** 간조 *kanjo*
low-fat 저지방 *chŏjibang*
luck 행운 *haengun*
lucky: to be lucky 운이 좋아요
un-i choayo
luggage 짐 *chim*, 수하물 *suhamul*
lukewarm 미지근해요
mijigŭnhaeyo
lunch 점심 *chŏmshim*; **to have
lunch** 점심 먹어요 *chŏmshim
mŏgŏyo*
lung 폐 *p'e*, 허파 *hŏp'a*
luxury (n) 고급품 *kogŭpp'um*
luxury (adj) 고급스러운
kogŭpsŭrŏun

M

magazine 잡지 *chapchi*
mail 우편 *up'yŏn*
main 주된 *chudwen*; **main course**
메인코스 *meink'osŭ*
make 만들어요 *mandŭrŏyo*
man 남자 *namja*
manage 관리해요 *kwallihaeyo*
manager 매니저 *maenijŏ*
many 많아요 *manayo*; **how many
...?** (things) ... 몇 개에요? *...
myŏt gae-eyo?*; (people) ... 몇 분
이에요? *... myŏt pun-ieyo*; **how
many times ...?** 몇 번 ...?
myŏt pŏn ...?
map 지도 *chido* **16, 33, 69, 76**

March 3월 sam-wol
market 시장 shijang **93**
married 결혼했어요
   kyŏlonhaessŏyo
mass 매스 maesŭ
match (for fire) 성냥 sŏngnyang
material 재료 chaeryo
matter: it doesn't matter 상관없
   어요 sanggwan-ŏpsŏyo
mattress 매트리스 maet'ŭrisŭ
May 5월 o-wol
maybe 아마 ama
me (polite) 저 chŏ; (informal) 나 na;
   me too 저도요 chŏ-do-yo
meal 식사 shiksa
mean 의미 uimi; **what does …
   mean?** … 무슨 의미에요? …
   musŭn uimi-eyo?
medicine 약 yak
medium 중간 chunggan; (meat) 미
   디엄 midiŏm
meet 만나요 mannayo **69**
meeting 회의 hwei
member 회원 hwewon
memory card 메모리 카드
   memori k'adŭ
menu 메뉴 menyu
message 메세지 meseji
meter 미터 mit'ŏ
metre 미터 mit'ŏ
microwave 전자레인지
   chŏnjareinji
midday 정오 chŏngo
middle 중간 chunggan; **in the
   middle (of)** … 의 중간에 … ui
   chunggan-e
midnight 자정 chajŏng
might: it might rain 비가 올지도
   몰라요 pi-ga oljido mollayo

mind: I don't mind 괜찮아요
   kwaench'anayo
mineral water 광천수
   kwangch'ŏnsu
minister 장관 changgwan
minute 분 bun; **at the last
   minute** 마지막 순간에 majimak
   sungan-e
mirror 거울 kŏul
Miss 미스 … misŭ …, … 씨 …
   ssi
miss 놓쳐요 noch'yŏyo; **we missed
   the train** 기차를 놓쳤어
   요 kich'a-rŭl noch'yŏssŏyo; **to be
   missing** … 없어요 … ŏpsŏyo
mistake 실수 shilsu; **to make a
   mistake** 실수를 해요 shilsu-rŭl
   haeyo
mobile (phone) 휴대전화 hyudae-
   chŏnhwa, 핸드폰 haendŭp'on **111**
modern 근대 kŭndae
moisturizer 모이스처크림
   moisŭch'ŏ-k'ŭrim
moment 순간 sungan; **at the
   moment** 지금 chigŭm
monastery 수도원 sudowon
Monday 월요일 wolyoil
money 돈 ton **91**
month 달 tal, 월 wol
monument 기념비 kinyŏmbi
mood: to be in a good/bad mood
   기분이 좋아요／나빠요 kibun-i
   choayo/nappayo
moon 달 tal
moped 모페드 mop'edŭ
more 더 tŏ; **more than** … 보다
   더 … poda tŏ; **much more, a lot
   more** 아주 더 aju tŏ; **there's
   no more …** … 더 없어요 …

tŏ ŏpsŏyo
morning 아침 *ach'im*
mosquito 모기 *mogi*
most: the most 대부분 *taebubun*;
   most people 대부분 사람들
   taebubun saram-tŭl
mother 어머니 *ŏmŏni*
motorbike 오토바이 *ot'obai*
motorway 고속도로 *kosoktoro*
mountain 산 *san*; **mountain bike**
   마운틴 바이크 *maun'tin paik'ŭ*;
   mountain hut 산장 *sanjang*
mouse *(for computer)* 마우스
   mausŭ; *(animal)* 쥐 *chwi*
mouth 입 *ip*
movie 영화 *yŏnghwa*
MP3 player 엠피쓰리 *emp'issŭri*
Mr/Mrs *(to elder or new*
   acquaintance) ⋯ 선생님 *…*
   sŏnsaengnim; *(to acquaintance of*
   similar age) ⋯ 씨 *… -sshi*
much: how much? 얼마 *ŏlma*;
   how much is it?, how much
   does it cost? 얼마에요? *ŏlma-*
   eyo?
muscle 근육 *kŭnyuk*
museum 박물관 *pangmulgwan*
music 음악 *ŭmak*
must ⋯ 해야 돼요 *… haeya*
   twaeyo; **I must go** 가야 돼요
   kaya twaeyo; **it must be 5 o'clock**
   5시일 거에요 *tasot-shi-il kŏ-eyo*
my *(polite)* 제 *che*; *(informal)* 내 *nae*

N

nail 손톱 *sont'op*
naked 나체 *nach'e*
name *(polite, when asking someone*

else) 성함 *sŏngham*; *(informal and*
for giving your own name) 이름
irŭm **41**; **what's your name ?** 성
함이 어떻게 되세요? *sŏngham-i*
ŏttŏk'e tweseyo?; **my name is …**
제 이름은 ⋯ 이에요 *che irŭm-*
ŭn … -ieyo
nap 낮잠 *natcham*; **to have a nap**
   낮잠을 자요 *natcham-ŭl chayo*
napkin 냅킨 *naepk'in*
nappy 기저귀 *jijŏgwi*
national holiday 국경일 *kukkyŏngil*
nature 자연 *chayŏn*
near 가까워요 *kakkawoyo*; **near**
   the beach 해변에서 가까워
   요 *haebyŏn-esŏ kakkawoyo*; **the**
   nearest … 가장 가까운 ⋯
   kajang kakkaun …
necessary 필요해요 *p'iyohaeyo*
neck 목 *mok*
need 필요해요 *p'iyohaeyo*
neighbour 이웃 *iut*
neither 둘 다 아니에요 *tul ta*
   anieyo; **neither … nor …** ⋯ 도
   ⋯ 도 둘 다 아니에요 *… -to*
   … -to tul ta anieyo
never 결코 ⋯ 아니에요 *kyŏlk'o*
   … anieyo
new 새 *sae*; **New Year** 새해
   saehae
news 뉴스 *nyusŭ*
newspaper 신문 *shinmun*
newsstand 신문판매대
   shimmunp'anmaedae
next 다음 *taŭm*
nice 좋아요 *choayo*
night 밤 *pam* **43, 45, 47**
nightclub 나이트 (클럽) *nait'ŭ*
   (k'ŭllŏp)

nightdress 잠옷 *chamot*
no 아니요 *aniyo*; **no, thank
you** 아니요, 괜찮아요 *aniyo
kwaench'anayo*; **no idea** 몰라요
mollayo
nobody 아무도 *amudo*
noise 소음 *soŭm*; **to make a noise**
소음을 내요 *soŭm-ŭl naeyo*
noisy 시끄러워요 *shikkŭrŏwoyo*
non-drinking water 마실 수 없
는 물 *mashil su ŏmnŭn mul*
none 아무도 *amudo*
non-smoker 비흡연자 *pihŭbyŏnja*
noon 정오 *chŏngo*
north 북쪽 *puktchok*; **in the north**
북쪽에 *puktchok-e*; **(to the)
north of** … (의) 북쪽에 …
(-e) puktchok-e
nose 코 *k'o*
not 아니에요 *anieyo*; **not yet** 아
직 아니에요 *ajik anieyo*; **not
at all** … 전혀 … 아니에요
chŏnhyŏ … anieyo
note 메모 *memo*
notebook 공책 *kongch'aek*
nothing 아무것도 *amugŏt-to*
novel 소설 *sosŏl*
November 11월 *ship-il-wol*
now 지금 *chigŭm*
nowadays 요즘 *yojŭm*
nowhere 아무데도 *amudedo*
number 숫자 *sutcha*
nurse 간호원 *kanhowon*

O

obvious 분명해요 *punmyŏnghaeyo*
ocean 대양 *taeyang*
o'clock: one o'clock … 시 … *-shi*;

three o'clock 3시 *se-shi*
October 10월 *shi-wol*
offer 제공해요 *chegonghaeyo*
often 가끔 *kakkŭm*
oil 기름 *kirŭm*
ointment 연고 *yŏngo*
OK 괜찮아요 *kwaench'anayo*
old (object) 오래됐어요
oraedwaessŏyo; (person) 나이 들었
어요 *nai tŭrŏssŏyo*; **how old are
you?** 나이가 어떻게 되세요? *
nai-ga ŏttŏk'e tweseyo?*; **old people**
노인 *noin*
on … 에 …*-e*
once 한번 *han-bŏn*; **once a day/an
hour** 하루/한 시간에 한번
haru/han shigan-e han-bŏn
one 하나 *hana*
only … 만 … *man*
open (adj) 열려 있어요 *yŏllyŏ
issŏyo*
open (v) 열어요 *yŏrŏyo*
operate 작용해요 *chagyonghaeyo*
operation: to have an operation
수술해요 *susulhaeyo*
opinion 의견 *uigyŏn*; **in my
opinion** 제 의견에는 *che
uigyŏn-e-nŭn*
opportunity 기회 *kihwe*
opposite (n) 반대 *pandae*
opposite (prep) … (의) 건너편에
… *(-e) kŏnnŏp'yŏn-e*
optician 안경사 *angyŏngsa*
or 또는 *tto-nŭn*
orange 오렌지 *orenji*
orchestra 오케스트라 *ok'esŭt'ŭra*
order: out of order 고장 *kojang*
order (v) 주문해요 *chumunhaeyo*
52, 90

organic 무농약 *munongyak*
organize 조직해요 *chojik'aeyo*
other 다른 *tarŭn*; **others** 다른 사람들 *tarŭn saram-tŭl*
otherwise 그렇지 않으면 *kŭrŏch'i anŭmyŏn*
our 우리 *uri*
outside 밖 *pakk*
oven 오븐 *obŭn*
over … 위에 *… wi-e*; **over there** 저기 *chŏgi*
overdone 너무 구웠어요 *nŏmu kuwŏssŏyo*
overweight (luggage etc) 중량초과 *chungnyangch'ogwa*
owe … 한테 빚지고 있어요 *… hant'e pit-chigo issŏyo* **55, 92**
own (v) 소유해요 *soyuhaeyo*
owner 소유자 *soyuja*

P

Pacific Ocean 태평양 *t'aep'yŏngyang*
pack: to pack one's suitcase 가방을 싸요 *kabang-ŭl ssayo*
packed 꽉 찼어요 *kkwak ch'assŏyo*
packet (parcel) 소포 *sop'o*
painting 회화 *hwehwa*, 미술 *misul*
palace 궁전 *kungjŏn*
pants 바지 *paji*
paper 종이 *chongi*; **paper napkin** 냅킨 *naepk'in*; **paper tissue** 티슈 *t'ishyu*
parcel 소포 *sopo*
pardon? 네? *ney?*
parents 부모님 *pumonim*
park (n) 공원 *kongwon*
park (v) 주차해요 *chuch'ahaeyo*

parking space 주차 공간 *chuch'a konggan*
part 부분 *pubun*; **to be a part of** … (의) 일부에요 *… (ui) ilbu-eyo*
party 파티 *p'at'i*
pass (n) 패스 *p'aesŭ*
pass (v) 지나가요 *chinagayo*
passenger 승객 *sŭnggaek*
passport 여권 *yŏgwon*
path 길 *kil*
patient (n) 환자 *hwanja*
pay (돈을) 내요 *(ton-ŭl) naeyo* **92, 109**
pedestrian 보행자 *pohaengja*
pedestrianized street 보행자 도로 *pohaengja toro*
pee 소변을 봐요 *sobyŏn-ŭl payo*
peel 껍질을 벗겨요 *kkŏpchil-ŭl pŏkkyŏyo*
pen 펜 *p'en*
pencil 연필 *yŏmp'il*
people 사람(들) *saram(-tŭl)* **51**
percent 퍼센트 *p'ŏsent'ŭ*
perfect 완벽해요 *wambyŏk'aeyo*
perfume 향수 *hyangsu*
perhaps 아마도 *amado*
period (menstruation) 생리 *saengni*
person 사람 *saram*
personal stereo 워크맨 *wok'ŭmaen*
petrol 기름 *kirŭm*, 휘발유 *hwibaryu*; **petrol station** 주유소 *chuyuso*
phone (n) 전화 *chŏnhwa*; **phone box** 공중전화 *kongjung- chŏnhwa* **111**; **phone call** 전화 *chŏnhwa*; **to make a phone call** 전화해요 *chŏnhwa-haeyo*; **phone number** 전화번호 *chŏnhwa-bŏnho*
phone (v) 전화해요 *chŏnhwa-haeyo*

phonecard 전화카드 chŏnhwa-k'adŭ **111**

photo 사진 sajin; **to take a photo (of)** … 사진을 찍어요 … sajin-ŭl tchikŏyo **99**

picnic 소풍 sop'ung; **to have a picnic** 소풍 가요 sop'ung kayo

pie 파이 p'ai

piece 조각 chogak; **a piece of** … 한 조각 … han chogak

piles 치질 ch'ijil

pill 피임약 p'iimyak; **to be on the pill** 피임약을 먹고 있어요 p'iimyak-ŭl mŏkko issŏyo

pillow 베개 pegae

pillowcase 베갯닛 pegaenit

PIN (number) 비밀번호 pimilbŏnho

pink 핑크 p'ingk'ŭ

pity: it's a pity 아까워요 akkawoyo

place 장소 changso

plan 계획 kehwek

plane 비행기 pihaenggi

plant 식물 shingmul

plaster (cast) 기브스 kibŭsŭ

plastic 프라스틱 p'ŭrasŭt'ik; **plastic bag** 비닐 봉투 pinil pongt'u

plate 접시 chŏpshi

platform 플랫폼 p'ŭlaepp'om **33**

play (n) 연극 yŏngŭk

play (v) (sport, game) … 해요 … haeyo **86**

please 부탁합니다 put'ak'amnida

pleased 기뻐요 kippŏyo; **pleased to meet you!** 만나서 반갑습니다 mannasŏ pangapsŭmnida

pleasure 기쁨 kippŭm

plug 플러그 p'ŭllŏgŭ

plug in 플러그를 꽂아요 p'ŭllŏgŭ-rŭl kkojayo

plumber 배관공 paegwangong

point 점 chŏm

police 경찰 kyŏngch'al; **police station** 경찰서 kyŏngch'alsŏ **125**

policeman 경찰관 kyŏngch'algwan

policewoman 경찰관 kyŏngch'algwan

poor 가난해요 kananhaeyo

port 항구 hanggu

portrait 초상화 ch'osanghwa

possible 가능해요 kanŭnghaeyo

post 우편 up'yŏn; **post office** 우체국 uch'eguk **105, 106**

postbox 우체통 uch'et'ong **105**

postcard 엽서 yŏpsŏ

postcode 우편번호 up'yŏn-bŏnho

poster 포스터 p'osŭt'ŏ

postman 우편배달부 up'yŏn-paedalbu

pot 주전자 chujŏnja

pound 파운드 p'aundŭ

powder 가루 karu

practical 실용적 siryongjŏk

pram 유모차 yumoch'a

prefer 더 좋아해요 tŏ choahaeyo

pregnant 임신했어요 imshinhaessŏyo **120**

prepare 준비해요 chumbihaeyo

present 선물 sŏmmul **97**

press 언론 ŏllon

pressure 압력 amnyŏk

previous 이전 ijŏn

price 값 kaps, 가격 kagyŏk

private (personal) 개인 kaein

prize 상 sang

probably 아마도 amado

problem 문제 munje

procession 행진 *haengjin*
product 제품 *chep'um*
profession 직업 *chigŏp*
programme 프로그램 *p'ŭrogŭraem*
promise 약속 *yaksok*
propose (suggest) 제안해요
   cheanhaeyo; (marriage) 청혼해요
   ch'ŏnghonhaeyo
protect 보호해요 *pohohaeyo*
public 공적이에요 *kongjŏk-ieyo*;
   public holiday 공휴일 *konghyuil*
pull 끌어요 *kkŭrŏyo*
purple 자색 *chasaek*
purpose 목적 *mokchŏk*; on
   purpose 일부러 *ilpurŏ*
purse 지갑 *chigap*
push 밀어요 *mirŏyo*
pushchair 유모차 *yumoch'a*
put 놓아요 *noayo*
put out 꺼요 *kkŏyo*
put up 올려요 *ollyŏyo*
put up with 참아요 *ch'amayo*

Q

quality 품질 *p'umjil*; of good/bad
   quality 품질이 좋아요／나빠
   요 *p'umjil-i choayo/nappayo*
quarter 사분의 일 *sa-bun-e il*;
   a quarter of an hour 십오 분
   ship-o pun; a quarter to ten 열시
   십오 분전 *yŏl-shi ship-o pun-chŏn*
quay 선창 *sŏnch'ang*
question 질문 *chilmun*
queue (n) 줄 *chul*
queue (v) 줄 서요 *chul sŏyo*
quick 빨라요 *ppallayo*
quickly 빨리 *ppalli*
quiet 조용해요 *choyonghaeyo*

quite 꽤 *kkwae*; quite a lot 꽤 많
   아요 *kkwae manayo*

R

racist 인종차별주의자
   injongch'abyŏljuuija
racket 라켓 *rak'et*
radiator 래디에이터 *raedieit'ŏ*
radio 라디오 *radio*; radio station
   라디오 방송국 *radio pangsongguk*
rain: it's raining 비가 와요 *pi-ga
   wayo*
raincoat 비옷 *pi-ot*
random: at random 무작위로
   mujagwi-ro
rape 강간 *kanggan*
rare 드물어요 *tŭmurŏyo*; (meat) 래
   어 *raeŏ*
rarely 드물게 *tŭmulge*
rather 오히려 *ohiryŏ*
raw 생 *saeng*
razor 면도기 *myŏndogi*; razor
   blade 면도날 *myŏndonal*
reach 도달해요 *todalhaeyo*
read 읽어요 *ilkŏyo*
ready 준비됐어요 *chumbitwessŏyo*
reasonable 적당해요
   chŏktanghaeyo
receipt 영수증 *yŏngsujŭng* 92
receive 받아요 *padayo*
reception 리셉션 *risepshyŏn*; at
   reception 리셉션 데스크에
   risepshyŏn tesŭk'ŭ-e
receptionist 안내원 *annaewon*
recipe 요리법 *yoribŏp*
recognize 인식해요 *inshik'aeyo*
recommend 추천해요
   ch'uch'ŏnhaeyo 50

red 빨개요 *ppalgaeyo*; **red light** 적신호 *chŏkshinho*; **red wine** 레드와인 *redŭ-wain* , 적포도주 *chŏkp'odoju*

reduce 줄여요 *chulyŏyo*

reduction 할인 *harin*

refrigerator 냉장고 *naengjanggo*

refund (n) 환불 *hwambul*; **to get a refund** 환불 받아요 *hwambul padayo* **96**

refund (v) 환불해요 *hwambulhaeyo*

refuse 거절해요 *kŏjŏlhaeyo*

registered 등록 됐어요 *tŭngnoktwessŏyo*

registration number 등록번호 *tŭngnok-pŏnho*

remember 기억해요 *kiŏk'aeyo*

remind 상기해요 *sanggihaeyo*

remove 제거해요 *chegŏhaeyo*

rent (n) 렌트 *rentŭ*

rent (v) 렌트해요 *rentŭ-haeyo*, 빌려요 *pillyŏyo*

rental 임대 *imdae*

reopen 재개해요 *chaegaehaeyo*, 다시 열어요 *tashi yŏrŏyo*

repair 수리해요 *surihaeyo* **36**

repeat 반복 *pambok* **14**

reserve 예약해요 *yeyak'aeyo* **51**

reserved 예약석 *yeyaksŏk*

rest: (n) **the rest** 나머지 *namoji*

rest (v) 쉬어요 *swiŏyo*

restaurant 식당 *shiktang* **50**

return 돌아가요 *tŭragayo*; **return ticket** 왕복표 *wangbokp'yo*

reverse-charge call 콜렉트콜 *k'ollekt'ŭ-k'ol* **111**

reverse gear 후진기어 *hujin-giŏ*

rheumatism 관절염 *kwanjŏlyŏm*

rib 갈비 *kalbi*

right (n) (not left) 오른쪽 *orŭntchok*; (entitlement) 권리 *kwolli*; **to the right (of)** … (의) 오른쪽에 *…(-e) orŭntchok-e*; **to have the right to ...** … 권리가 있어요 *… kwolli-ga issŏyo*

right (adj) **that's right!** 맞아요! *majayo!*

right (adv) **right away** 바로 *paro*; **right beside** 바로 옆에 *paro yŏp'-e*

ring 반지 *panji*

ripe 익었어요 *igŏssŏyo*

rip off: to get ripped off 바가지 써요 *pagaji ssŏyo*

risk 위험 *wihŏm*

river 강 *kang*

road 길 *kil*, 도로 *toro*; **road sign** 도로 표지 *toro p'yoji*

rock 바위 *pawi*

room 방 *pang* **43, 44**

rosé wine 로제와인 *roje-wain*

round 둥근 *tunggŭn*

rubbish 쓰레기 *ssŭregi*; **to take the rubbish out** 쓰레기를 버려요 *ssŭregi-rŭl pŏryŏyo*

rucksack 배낭 *paenang*

rug 담요 *damyo*

ruins 폐허 *p'ehŏ*; **in ruins** 폐허가 됐어요 *p'ehŏ-ga twaessŏyo*

run 떨어져요 *ttŏrŏjyŏyo*

run out 달려요 *tallyŏyo*; **to have run out of petrol** 기름이 떨어졌어요 *kirŭm-i tŏrŏjyŏssŏyo*

S

sad 슬퍼요 *sŭlp'ŏyo*

safe 안전해요 *anjŏnhaeyo*
safety 안전 *anjŏn*; **safety belt** 안전띠 *anjŏn-tti*
sail 항해해요 *hanghaehaeyo*
sale 세일 *seil*; **in the sale** 세일로 *seil-lo*
salt 소금 *sogŭm*
salted 소금간 *sogŭmgan*
salty 짜요 *tchayo*
same 같아요 *kat'ayo*
sand 모래 *morae*
sandals 샌들 *saendŭl*
sanitary towel 생리대 *saengnidae*
Saturday 토요일 *t'oyoil*
saucepan 냄비 *naembi*
save 저축해요 *chŏch'uk'aeyo*
say 말해요 *malhaeyo*; **how do you say... ?** 어떻게 말해요? ... *ŏttŏk'e malhaeyo?*
scared: to be scared (of) 무서워요 *musŏwoyo*
scenery 경치 *kyŏngch'i*
scissors 가위 *kawi*
scoop: one/two scoop(s) (of ice cream) 한／두 스푼*han/tu sŭp'un*
scooter 스쿠터 *sŭk'ut'ŏ*
scotch (whisky) 위스키 *wisŭk'i*
Scotland 스코틀랜드 *sŭk'ot'ŭllaendŭ*
Scotsman, Scotswoman스코틀랜드 사람 *sŭk'ot'ŭllaendŭ saram*
scuba diving 스쿠버 다이빙 *sŭk'ubŏ taibing*
sea 바다 *pada*
seafood 해산물 *haesammul*
seasick: to be seasick 배멀미해요 *paemŏlmi-haeyo*
seaside 해변 *haebyŏn*
season 계절 *kejŏl*

seat 자리 *chari* **28**
seaweed 해초 *haech'o*
second 둘째 *tul-tchae*; **second class** 이류 *iryu*
second-hand 중고 *chunggo*
secure 안전해요 *anjŏnhaeyo*
security 안전 *anjŏn*
see 봐요 *payo*; **see you later!** (formal) 나중에 봐요! *najung-e payo!*; (informal)뵙겠습니다! *pekkessŭmnida!*; **see you soon!** (formal) 또 봐요! *tto payo!*; (informal)뵙겠습니다! *pekkessŭmnida!*;
see you tomorrow! (formal) 내일 봐요! *naeil payo!*; (informal)뵙겠습니다! *pekkessŭmnida!*
seem … 같아요 *... kat'ayo*; **it seems that ...** … 인 거 같아요 *... in kŏ kat'ayo*
seldom 가끔 *kakkŭm*
sell 팔아요 *p'arayo*
Sellotape® 스카치테입 *sŭk'ach'it'eip*
send 보내요 *ponaeyo*
sender 보내는 사람 *ponae-nŭn saram*
sense 감각 *kamgak*
sentence 문장 *munjang*
separate 갈라요 *kallayo*
separately 따로 *ttaro*
September 9월 *ku-wol*
serious 심각해요 *shimgak'aeyo*
several 여러 *yŏrŏ*
sex 성 *sŏng*
shade 그늘 *kŭnŭl*; **in the shade** 그늘에 *kŭnŭl-e*
shampoo 샴푸 *shyamp'u*
shape 모양 *moyang*

share 나눠요 *nanwoyo*

shave 면도해요 *myŏndohaeyo*

shaving: shaving cream 면도 크림 *myŏndo k'ŭrim*; **shaving foam** 면도 거품 *myŏndo kŏp'um*

she 그 여자 *kŭ yŏja*

sheet 시트 *shit'ŭ*

shellfish 조개 *chogae*

shirt 셔츠 *shyŏch'ŭ*

shock 충격 *ch'unggyŏk*

shocking 충격적이에요 *ch'unggyŏk-chŏk-ieyo*

shoes 신발 *shimbal*

shop 가게 *kage*; **shop assistant** 점원 *chŏmwon*

shopkeeper 가게 주인 *kage chuin*

shopping 쇼핑 *shyop'ing*; **to go shopping** 쇼핑 해요 *shyop'ing haeyo*; **shopping centre** 쇼핑센터 *shyop'ing-sent'ŏ*

short 작아요 *chagayo*; **short cut** 지름길 *chirŭmgil*

shorts 반바지 *pan-paji*

short-sleeved 반팔 *pan-p'al*

shoulder 어깨 *okkae*

show (n) 쇼 *shyo*

show (v) 보여 줘요 *poyŏ chŏyo*

shower 샤워 *shyawo*; **to take a shower** 샤워 해요 *shyawo haeyo*; **shower gel** 샤워 젤 *shyawo jel*

shut 닫아요 *tadayo*

shuttle 셔틀 *shyŏt'ŭl*

shy 소심해요 *soshimhaeyo*

sick: to feel sick 속이 안 좋아요 *sok-i an choayo*

side 옆 *yŏp*

sign (n) 표지 *p'yoji*

sign (v) 싸인해요 *ssain-haeyo*

signal 신호 *shinho*

silent 조용해요 *choyonghaeyo*

silver 은 *ŭn*

silver-plated 은도금 *ŭndogŭm*

since … 부터 … *put'ŏ*

sing 노래해요 *noraehaeyo*

singer 가수 *kasu*

single (adj) 싱글 *shinggŭl*

single (ticket) 편도 *p'yŏndo*

sister (elder sister of female) 언니 *ŏnni*; (elder sister of male) 누나 *nuna*; (younger sister) 여동생 *yŏ-dongsaeng*

sit down 앉아요 *anjayo*

size 크기 *k'ŭgi*

ski 스키 *sŭk'i* **85; ski boots** 스키화 *sŭk'i-hwa*; **ski lift** 스키 리프트 *sŭk'i rip'ŭt'ŭ*; **ski pole** 스키폴 *sŭk'i p'ol*; **ski resort** 스키장 *sŭk'i-jang*

skiing 스키 *sŭk'i*; **to go skiing** 스키 타요 *sŭk'i t'ayo*

skin 피부 *p'ibu*

skirt 치마 *ch'ima*

sky 하늘 *hanŭl*

skyscraper 고층건물 *koch'ŭng-kŏmmul*

sleep (n) 잠 *cham*

sleep (v) 자요 *chayo*; **to sleep with** … 하고 함께 자요 … *-hago hamkke chayo*

sleeping: sleeping bag 침낭 *ch'imnang*; **sleeping pill** 수면제 *sumyŏnje*

sleepy: to be sleepy 졸려요 *chollyŏyo*

sleeve 소매 *somae*

slice 조각 *chogak*

sliced 잘라냈어요 *challanaessŏyo*

slide 슬라이드 *sŭllaidŭ*

slow 느려요 *nŭryŏyo*

slowly 느리게 *nŭrige*

small 작아요 *chagayo*

smell (n) 냄새 *naemsae*

smell (v) 냄새 나요 *naemsae nayo*; **to smell good/bad** 냄새 좋아요／나빠요 *naemsae choayo/nappayo*

smoke 담배를 피워요 *tambae-rŭl p'iwoyo*

smoker 흡연자 *hŭbyŏnja*

snack 간식 *kanshik*

snow (n) 눈 *nun*

snow (v) 눈이 와요 *nun-i wayo*

so 그래서 *kŭraesŏ*; **so that** … 수 있도록 … *su ittorok*

soap 비누 *pinu*

soccer 축구 *ch'ukku*

socks 양말 *yangmal*

somebody, someone 어떤 사람 *ŏttŏn saram*

something 어떤 거 *ŏttŏn kŏ*; **something else** 다른 거 *tarŭn kŏ*

sometimes 때로는 *ttaero-nŭn*

somewhere 어딘가 *ŏdinga*

son 아들 *adŭl*

song 노래 *norae*

soon 곧 *kot*

sore 아파요 *ap'ayo*; **to have a sore throat** 목이 아파요 *mok-i ap'ayo*

sorry: I'm sorry 미안합니 다 *mianhamnida*, 죄송합니다 *chwesonghamnida*

south 남쪽 *namtchok*; **in the south** 남쪽에 *namtchok-e*; **(to the) south of** … (의) 남쪽에

… (-e) namtchok-e

souvenir 기념품 *kinyŏmp'um*

spare 남아요 *namayo*; **spare part** 예비 부품 *yebi pup'um*; **spare tyre** 스페어 타이어 *sŭp'eŏ t'aiŏ*; **spare wheel** 스페어 바퀴 *sŭp'eŏ pak'wi*

spark plug 스파크 플러그 *sŭp'ak'ŭ p'ŭllŏgŭ*

speak 말해요 *malhaeyo* **13, 14, 77, 112**

special 특별해요 *t'ŭkpyŏlhaeyo*

speciality 전문 *chŏnmun*

speed 속도 *sokto*; **at full speed** 제일 빠른 속도로 *jeil pparŭn sokto-ro*

spell 써요 *ssŏyo*; **how do you spell it?** 어떻게 써요? *ŏttŏk'e ssŏyo?*

spend (money) 써요 *ssŏyo*; (time) 보 내요 *ponaeyo*

spice 양념 *yangnyŏm*

spicy 매워요 *maewoyo*

spider 거미 *kŏmi*

split up 헤어져요 *heŏjyŏyo*

spoil 망쳐요 *mangch'yŏyo*

sponge 스펀지 *sŭp'ŏnji*

spoon 숟가락 *sukkarak*

sport 스포츠 *sŭp'och'ŭ*, 운동 *undong*

sports ground 운동장 *undong-jang*

sporty 운동 신경이 좋아요 *undong shingyŏng-i choayo*

spot 점 *chŏm*

sprain 뼈요 *ppyŏyo*; **to sprain one's ankle** 발목을 뼈요 *palmok-ŭl ppyŏyo*

spring 봄 *pom*

square 정사각형 *chŏngsagak'yŏng*

stadium 경기장 *kyŏnggijang*

stain 얼룩 *olluk*

stairs 계단 *kedan*

stamp 우표 *up'yo* **106**

start 시작해요 *shijak'aeyo*

state 상태 *sangt'ae*

statement 진술 *chinsul*

station 역 *yŏk*

stay (v) 머물러요 *mŏmullŏyo*; **to stay in touch** 계속 연락해요 *kesok yŏllak'aeyo*

steal 훔쳐요 *humch'yŏyo*

steps 계단 *kedan*

sticking plaster 반창고 *panch'anggo*

still (adv) 아직도 *ajik-to*

still water 무탄산수 *mut'ansansu*

sting (v) 물어요 *murŏyo*

stock: out of stock 다 떨어졌어요 *ta ttŏrŏjyŏssŏyo*

stomach 배 *pae*

stone 돌 *tol*

stop (n) 정거장 *chŏngŏjang*

stop (v) 멈춰요 *mŏmch'ŏyo*

stopcock 마개 *magae*

storey 층 *ch'ŭng*

storm 폭풍 *p'okp'ung*

straight ahead, straight on 직진 *chikchin*

strange 이상해요 *isanghaeyo*

street 거리 *kŏri*

strong 강해요 *kanghaeyo*

stuck 움직이지 않아요 *umjikiji anayo*

student 학생 *haksaeng* **28**

studies 공부 *kongbu*

study 공부해요 *kongbu-haeyo*; **to study biology** 생물을 공부해요 *saengmul-ŭl kongbu-haeyo*

style 스타일 *sŭt'ail*

subtitles 자막 *chamak*

suburb 교외 *kyo-e*

suffer 고생해요 *kosaenghaeyo*

suggest 제안해요 *cheanhaeyo*

suit (v) 양복 *yangbok*

suit (n) 어울려요 *ŏullyŏyo*

suitcase 여행가방 *yŏhaeng-kabang* **30**

summer 여름 *yŏrŭm*

summit 정상 *chŏngsang*

sun 해 *hae*; **in the sun** 햇볕에 *haeppyŏt-e*; **sun cream** 썬크림 *ssŏnk'ŭrim*

sunbathe 일광욕을 해요 *ilgwangyok-ŭl haeyo*

sunburnt: to get sunburnt 햇볕에 타요 *haeppyŏt-e t'ayo*

Sunday 일요일 *ilyoil*

sunglasses 썬글라스 *ssŏngŭllasŭ*

sunrise 일출 *ilch'ul*

sunset 일몰 *ilmol*

sunstroke 일사병 *ilsabyŏng*; **to get sunstroke** 일사병 걸렸어요 *ilsabyŏng kŏllyŏssŏyo*

supermarket 슈퍼(마켓) *sup'ŏ(mak'et)* **42**

supplement (charge) 추가요금 *ch'uga-yogŭm*

sure 확실해요 *hwakshilhaeyo*

surgical spirit 소독약 *sodok-yak*

surname 성 *sŏng*

surprised 놀래요 *nollaeyo*

sweat 땀 *ttam*

sweater 스웨터 *sŭwet'ŏ*

sweet (n) 사탕 *sat'ang*

sweet (adj) 달아요 *tarayo*

swim (v) 수영해요 *suyŏnghaeyo*

swimming 수영 *suyŏng*; **swimming pool** 수영장 *suyŏng-*

jang; **swimming trunks** 수영복 suyŏng-bok

swimsuit 수영복 suyŏng-bok

switch off 꺼요 kkŏyo

switch on 켜요 k'yŏyo

switchboard operator 교환원 kyohwanwon

swollen 부었어요 puŏssŏyo

syrup (medicine) 물약 mullyak

T

table 테이블 t'eibŭl **51**; (dining table) 식탁 shikt'ak

tablespoon 테이블 스푼 t'eibŭl sŭp'un

tablet 알약 al-lyak

take (object) 가져가요 kajyŏgayo; (medicine) 먹어요 mŏgŏyo; (time) 걸려요 kŏllyŏyo; **it takes two hours** 두 시간 걸려요 tu shigan kŏllyŏyo

take away 포장 p'ojang; **I'd like to take it away** 포장해 주세요 p'ojang-hae chuseyo

take off (plane) 이륙해요 iryuk'aeyo

talk 말해요 malhaeyo

tall (building) 높아요 nop'ayo; (person) 키가 커요 k'i-ga k'ŏyo

tampon 탐폰 t'amp'on

tan 햇볕에 타요 haeppyŏt'-e t'ayo

tanned 햇볕에 탔어요 haeppyŏt'-e t'assŏyo

tap 수도꼭지 sudo-kkokchi

taste (v) 맛 봐요 mat payo

taste (n) 맛 mat

tax 세금 segŭm

tax-free 면세 myŏnse

taxi 택시 t'aekshi **37**; **taxi driver** 택시기사 t'aekshi-kisa

team 팀 t'im

teaspoon 티스푼 t'isŭp'un

teenager 십대 shiptae

telephone (n) 전화기 chŏnhwagi

telephone (v) 전화해요 chŏnhwa-haeyo

television 텔레비전 t'ellebijŏn

tell 이야기해요 iyagihaeyo

temperature (of climate, room, etc) 온도 ondo; (of body) 체온 ch'eon; **to take one's temperature** 체온을 재요 ch'eon-ŭl chaeyo

temple 절 chŏl

temporary 일시적 ilshijŏk

tennis 테니스 t'enisŭ; **tennis court** 테니스장 t'enisŭ-jang; **tennis shoe** 테니스화 t'enisŭ-hwa

tent 텐트 t'ent'ŭ; **tent peg** 텐트 페그 t'ent'ŭ p'egŭ

terminal (at airport) 터미날 t'ŏminal

terrace 테라스 t'erasŭ

terrible 무시무시해요 mushimushihaeyo

thank: thank you, thanks 감사합니다 kamsahamnida, 고맙습니다 komapsŭmnida; **thanks to** … 덕분에 … tŏkbun-e

that, that one 그 거 ku kŏ

theatre 극장 kŭkchang

theft 도둑질 todukchil

theme park 놀이공원 nori-kongwon

then (at that time) 그 때 ku ttae; (afterwards) 그 다음에 kŭ taŭm-e

there 거기 kŏgi; **there is/there are …** … 있어요 … issŏyo

therefore 그러므로 kŭrŏmŭro

thermometer 온도계 *ondoge*

Thermos® flask 보온병 *po-onbyŏng*

these, these ones 이 거 *i kŏ*

they 그 사람들 *ku saram-tŭl*; **they say that …** …라고들 말해요 *… rago-tŭl malhaeyo*

thief 도둑 *toduk*

thigh 허벅지 *hŏbŏkchi*

thin (object) 얇아요 *yalbayo*; (person) 말랐어요 *mallassŏyo*

thing 물건 *mulgŏn*

think 생각해요 *saenggak'aeyo*

think about … 에 대해 생각해요 *…-e taehae saenggak'aeyo*

thirsty: to be thirsty 목말라요 *mog-mallayo*

this, this one 이 거 *i kŏ*; **this evening** 오늘 저녁 *onŭl chŏnyŏk*; **this is …** …이에요 *… ieyo*

those, those ones 저 거 *chŏ kŏ*

throat 목 *mok*

throw 던져요 *tŏnjyŏyo*

throw out 밖으로 던져요 *pakk-ŭro tŏnjyŏyo*

Thursday 목요일 *mogyoil*

ticket 표 *p'yo* **28, 71, 78**; **ticket office** 매표소 *maep'yoso*

tidy 깨끗해요 *kkaekkŭt'aeyo*

tie 묶어요 *mukkŏyo*

tight 촘촘해요 *ch'omch'omhaeyo*

tights 스타킹 *sŭt'ak'ing*

time 시간 *shigan*; **what time is it?** 몇시에요? *myŏ shi-eyo ?*; **from time to time** 때때로 *ttaettae-ro*; **on time** 시간 맞게 *shigan makke*; **three/four times** 세／네 번 *se/ne pŏn*; **time difference** 시차 *shich'a*

timetable 시간표 *shiganp'yo* **28**

tip 봉사료 *pongsaryo*

tired 피곤해요 *p'igonhaeyo*

tobacco 담배 *tambae*

today 오늘 *onŭl*

together 함께 *hamkke*

toilet 화장실 *hwajangshil* **13, 51**; **toilet bag** 화장품 가방 *hwajangp'um kabang*; **toilet paper** 화장지 *hwajangji*

toiletries 화장품 *hwajangp'um*

toll 통행료 *t'onghaengnyo*

tomorrow 내일 *naeil*; **tomorrow evening** 내일 저녁 *naeil chŏnyŏk*; **tomorrow morning** 내일 아침 *naeil ach'im*

tongue 혀 *hyŏ*

tonight 오늘 밤 *onŭl pam*

too 너무 *nŏmu*; **too many/much** 너무 많아요 *nŏmu manayo*

tooth 이빨 *ippal*

toothbrush 칫솔 *ch'issol*

toothpaste 치약 *ch'iyak*

top 꼭대기 *kkoktaegi*; **at the top** 꼭대기에 *kkoktaegi-e*

torch 손전등 *sonjŏndŭng*

touch 만져요 *manjyŏyo*

tourist 관광객 *kwanggwanggaek*; **tourist office** 관광 안내소 *kwanggwang annaeso* **76**; **tourist trap** 관광 명소 *kwanggwang myŏngso*

towards … 쪽으로 *… tchok-ŭro*

towel 수건 *sugŏn*

town 동네 *tongne*; **town centre** 시내 *shinae*; **town hall** 시청 *shich'ŏng*

toy 장난감 *changnangam*

traditional 전통적이에요

chŏnt'ongjŏk-ieyo

traffic 교통 *kyot'ong*; **traffic jam** 교통혼잡 *kyot'ong-honjap*

train 기차 *kich'a* **33, 34**; **the train to Seoul** 서울행 기차 *seoul-haeng kich'a*; **train station** (기차)역 *(kich'a-)yŏk*

tram 전차 *chŏnch'a*

transfer *(of money)* 송금 *songgŭm* **103**

translate 번역해요 *pŏnyŏk'aeyo*

travel 여행해요 *yŏhaeng-haeyo*; **travel agency** 여행사 *yŏhaengsa*

traveller's cheque 여행자 수표 *yŏhaengja sup'yo*

trip 여행 *yŏhaeng*; **have a good trip!** 여행 재미있게 하세요 *yŏhaeng chaemi-ikke haseyo*

trolley *(in supermarket)* 카트 *k'atŭ*

trouble 문제 *munje*

trousers 바지 *paji*

true 정말 *chŏngmal*

try … 시도해요 *… shidohaeyo*

try on 입어 봐요 *ibŏ payo* **95**

Tuesday 화요일 *hwayoil*

turn: *(n)* 차례 *ch'are*; **it's your turn** 그 쪽 차례입니다 *kŭ tchok ch'are-imnida*

turn *(v)* 돌아요 *torayo*

twice 두 번 *tu pŏn*

type *(n)* 유형 *yuhyŏng*

type *(v)* 타이프 쳐요 *t'aip'ŭ ch'yŏyo*

typical 전형적이에요 *chŏnhyŏngjŏk-ieyo*

tyre 타이어 *t'aiŏ*

U

umbrella 우산 *usan*

uncomfortable 불편해요 *pulp'yŏnhaeyo*

under 밑에 *mit'-e*

underground 지하철 *chihach'ŏl* **33**; **underground line** 지하철 노선 *chihach'ŏl nosŏn*; **underground station** 지하철역 *chihach'ŏl-yŏk*

underneath 아래 *arae*

understand *(what someone is saying)* 알아들어요 *ara-tŭrŏyo*; *(anything else)* 이해해요 *ihaehaeyo* **14**

underwear 속옷 *sok-ot*

United Kingdom 영국 *yŏngguk*

United States 미국 *miguk*

until … 까지 *… kkaji*

upset 속상해요 *soksanghaeyo*

upstairs 윗층 *wit-ch'ung*

urgent 급해요 *kŭp'aeyo*

us 우리 *uri*

use 사용해요 *sayonghaeyo*; **to be used for** … 위해서 사용해요 *… wihaesŏ sayonghaeyo*; **I'm used to** … 에 익숙해요 *… -e iksuk'aeyo*

useful 유용해요 *yuyonghaeyo*

useless 쓸모 없어요 *ssŭlmo ŏpsŏyo*

usually 보통 *pot'ong*

U-turn 유턴 *yu-t'ŏn*

V

vaccinated (against) … 에게 예방 접종을 했어요 *… ege yebang chŏpchong-ŭl haessŏyo*

valid 유효해요 *yuhyohaeyo*; **valid (for)** … 에 유효해요 *… -e yuhyohaeyo*

valley 골짜기 *koltchagi*

VAT 부가가치세 *pugagach'ise*
vegetarian 채식주의자
   ch'aeshikchuuija
very 아주 *aju*
view 전망 *chŏmmang*
village 마을 *maŭl*
visa 비자 *pija*
visit (n) 방문 *pangmun*
visit (v) 방문해요 *pangmun-haeyo*
volleyball 배구 *paegu*
vomit 토해요 *t'ohaeyo*

W

waist 허리 *hŏri*
wait 기다려요 *kidaryŏyo*; **to wait for** … 기다려요 … *kidaryŏyo*
waiter 웨이터 *weit'ŏ*
waitress 웨이트레스 *weit'ŭresŭ*
wake up 일어나요 *irŏnayo*
Wales 웨일스 *weilsŭ*
walk: (n) **to go for a walk** 산책해요 *sanch'aek'aeyo*
walk (v) 걸어요 *kŏroyo*
walking boots 등산화 *tŭngsanhwa*
Walkman® 워크맨 *wok'ŭmaen*
wallet 지갑 *chigap*
want: to want … 원해요 … *wonhaeyo*; **to want to do** … 하고 싶어요 … *hago ship'ŏyo*
warm 따뜻해요 *ttattŭt'aeyo*
warn 경고해요 *kyŏnggohaeyo*
wash: to have a wash 세수해요 *sesuhaeyo*
wash 닦아요 *ttakkayo*; **to wash one's hair** 머리를 감아요 *mŏri-rŭl kamayo*
washbasin 세수대야 *sesudaeya*
washing: to do the washing 빨

래해요 *ppallae-haeyo*; **washing machine** 세탁기 *set'akki*; **washing powder** 세제 *seje*; **washing-up liquid** 설거지 세제 *sŏlgŏji seje*
wasp 말벌 *malbŏl*
waste (v) 낭비해요 *nangbihaeyo*
watch (n) 시계 *shige*
watch (v) 지켜 봐요 *chik'yŏ payo*; **watch out!** 조심해요! *choshimhaeyo!*
water 물 *mul* 53; **water heater** 온수기 *onsugi*
waterproof (clothes) 방수복 *pangsubok*
waterskiing 수상스키 *susang-sŭk'i*
wave 파도 *p'ado*
way 길 *kil* 16
way in 입구 *ipku*
way out 출구 *ch'ulgu*
we 우리 *uri*
weak 약해요 *yak'aeyo*
wear 입어요 *ibŏyo*
weather 날씨 *nalsshi*; **the weather's bad** 날씨가 안 좋아요 *nalsshi-ga an choayo*; **weather forecast** 일기 예보 *ilki yebo*
website 웹사이트 *wep-saitŭ*
Wednesday 수요일 *suyoil*
week 일주일 *iljuil*
weekend 주말 *chumal*
welcome 환영해요 *hwanyŏnghaeyo*; **welcome!** 어서오세요! *ŏsŏ-oseyo!*; **you're welcome** 천만에요 *chŏnman-eyo*
well 잘 *chal*; **I'm very well** 잘 있어요 *chal issŏyo*; **well done** (meat) 잘 익힘 *chal ik'im*
well-known 유명해요

yumyŏnghaeyo

Welshman, Welshwoman 웨일스
사람 *weilsŭ saram*

west 서쪽 *sŏtchok*; **in the west** 서
쪽에 *sŏtchok-e*; **(to the) west of**
… (의) 서쪽 … *(-e) sŏtchok*

wet 젖었어요 *chŏjŏssŏyo*

what 무엇 *muŏt*; **what do you
want?** 무엇을 도와 드릴까요?
muŏs-ŭl towa tŭrilkkayo?

wheel 바퀴 *pak'wi*

wheelchair 휠체어 *hwilch'eŏ*

when 언제 *ŏnje*

where 어디 *ŏdi*; **where is/are …?**
… 어디 있어요? *… ŏdi issŏyo*;
where are you from? 어느 나
라 사람이세요? *ŏnu nara saram-
iseyo?*; **where are you going?** 어
디 가세요? *ŏdi kaseyo?*

which 어느 *ŏnŭ*

while … 동안 *… tongan*

white 하얀색 *hayansaek*; **white
wine** 화이트 와인 *hwait'ŭ wain*,
백포도주 *paekp'odoju*

who 누구 *nugu*; **who's calling?** 누
구세요? *nugu-seyo?*

whole 전체 *chŏnch'e*; **the whole
cake** 케이크 전부 *k'eik'ŭ
chŏmbu*

whose 누구(의) *nugu(-e)*

why 왜 *wae*

wide 넓어요 *nolbŏyo*

wife *(polite – someone else's)* 부인
puin; *(humble – one's own)* 집사람
chip-saram

wild 야생 *yasaeng*

wind 바람 *param*

window 창문 *ch'angmun*

windscreen 앞 유리 *ap yuri*

wine 와인 *wain*, 포도주 *p'odoju*
53

winter 겨울 *kyŏul*

with … 하고 같이 *… hago kach'i*

withdraw 인출해요 *inch'ulhaeyo*

without … 없이 *… ŏpshi*

woman 여자 *yŏja*

wonderful 훌륭해요 *hullyunghaeyo*

wood *(timber)* 나무 *namu*; *(forest)*
숲 *sup*

wool 양털 *yangt'ŏl*

work *(n) (job)* 일 *il*; **work of art** 작
품 *chakp'um*

work *(v)* 일해요 *ilhaeyo*

world 세계 *sege*

worse 더 나빠요 *tŏ nappayo*;
to get worse 악화돼요
yak'watwaeyo; **it's worse (than)**
… 보다 더 나빠요 *… poda tŏ
nappayo*

worth: to be worth 가치 *kach'i*;
it's worth it 가치 있어요 *kach'i
issŏyo*

wound 상처 *sangch'ŏ*

wrist 손목 *sommok*

write 써요 *ssŏyo* **15, 92**

wrong 틀려요 *t'ŭllyŏyo*

X

X-rays 엑스레이 *eksŭ-rei*

Y

year 해 *hae*, 년 *nyŏn*

yellow 노란색 *noransaek*

yes 네 *ne*

yesterday 어제 *ŏje*; **yesterday
evening** 어제 저녁 *ŏje chŏnyŏk*

you 너 *nŏ* *(only used to close friends*

of similar age; otherwise use name or title)
young (*child*) 어려요 *ŏryŏyo*; (*adult*) 젊어요 *chŏlmŏyo*
your 네 *ne* (*only used to close friends of similar age; otherwise use name or title followed by* 의 *-e*)

youth hostel 유스 호스텔 *yusŭ hosŭt'el*

zip 지퍼 *chip'ŏ*
zoo 동물원 *tongmulwon*
zoom (lens) 줌렌즈 *chum-renjŭ*

GRAMMAR

Spoken by around 72 million people in North and South Korea and by large ethnic Korean communities overseas (mainly in China, Japan, the USA and Central Asia), Korean is thought by some linguists to be a member of the Altaic language family. This would make it related to Turkish, Mongolian and Manchu. In terms of grammar, Korean actually has much more in common with Japanese; however, no genealogical link has been determined between the two languages. It should also be noted that although Korean contains a lot of vocabulary of Chinese origin, it is in no way related to Chinese and the grammars of the two languages could hardly be more different.

Word order

The basic word order of Korean differs from that of English. Whereas English typically follows the pattern of subject-verb-object, Korean is usually subject-object-verb. Therefore, while English speakers will say "Su-mi ate kimchi", Korean speakers will say "Su-mi kimchi ate", or 수미가 김치를 먹었어요 *Su-mi-ga kimch'i-rul mŏgŏssŏyo*, to be more precise.

Another difference between Korean and English word order is that whereas the latter has prepositions, the former has postpositions. In other words, whereas English speakers say "at home" and "by bus", Korean speakers say "home-at" and "bus-by" – 집에 *chip-e* and 버스로 *pŏsŭ-ro*.

Word dropping

Unlike English, Korean is a language in which words in the sentence – including the subject and object – can often be dropped when who or what you are talking about is obvious from the context. For example, while in English it is unusual to drop the "I" in sentences such as "I ate kimchi" even when it is clear that you are talking about yourself, in Korean it is common just to say "kimchi ate" 김치 먹었어요 *kimch'i mŏgŏssŏyo* as long as it is obvious that you are talking about yourself.

In informal language, postpositions and other particles (see below) are also often dropped. For example, it is possible to say "I went to school" just as 학교 갔어요 *hakkyo kassŏyo* (literally "school went") with no equivalent of the preposition "to" (in Korean 에 -e) at all. However, in formal and written language particles are always maintained.

Nouns and particles

Korean has a system of particles – endings that attach to nouns to express the grammatical role of the noun or else to add focus or emphasis. The following table lists the most common of these particles and describes their function. Note that some particles have a different form depending on whether the word they attach to ends in a consonant or a vowel

Particle		Basic Function	Examples
After Cons.	**After Vowel**		
이 -i	가 -ga	**Subject Marker**: marks the noun as the grammatical subject of the sentence	민호가 왔어요 *Min-ho-ga wassŏyo* Min-ho-(*subject*) has come
을 -ŭl	를 -rŭl	**Object Marker**: marks the noun as the grammatical object of the sentence	민호가 담배를 피워요 *Min-ho-ga tambae-rŭl piwoyo* Min-ho-(subject) smokes cigarettes-(*object*)
은 -ŭn	는 -nŭn	**Topic Marker**: (1) "backgrounds" a noun as the topic of a sentence; (2) shows contrast between two nouns	민호는 가지만 수미는 안 가요 *Min-ho-nŭn kajiman Su-mi-nŭn an kayo* Min-ho-(*topic*) is going, but Su-mi-(*topic*) is not
의 -e		**Possessive**: just like the possessive marker **'s** in English	민호의 김치에요 *Min-ho-e kimch'i-eyo* it's Min-ho's kimchi

에 -e	**Postposition of location and direction**: (1) used like "at" when talking about something being statically at a location; (2) used like "to", when talking about going towards somewhere	학교에 있어요 *hakkyo-e issŏyo* ... is at school 학교에 가요 *hakkyo-e kayo* ... goes to school
에서 -esŏ	**Postposition of location and direction**: (1) used like "at" when talking about doing something actively at a location; (2) used like "from", when talking about coming from somewhere	학교에서 공부해요 *hakkyo-esŏ kongbuhaeyo* ... studies at school 영국에서 왔어요 *yŏngguk-esŏ wassŏyo* ... comes from the UK
한테 -hant'e 에게 -ege	**Postpositions of direction**: used like "to" when talking about giving, sending, etc something to someone	수미한테 보내요 *Su-mi-hant'e ponaeyo* ... send to Su-mi
한테(서) 에게(서)	**Postpositions of direction**: used like "from" when talking about receiving, etc to someone	민호한테서 받아요 *Min-ho-hant'esŏ padayo* ... receives from Min-ho
하고 *hago*	**"and", "with"**	포도주하고 맥주 *p'ogoju-hago maekchu* wine and beer
도 -to	**"too", "also"**	수미도 가요 *Su-mi-to kayo* Su-mi is going too

| 들 -tŭl | **Plural marker**: makes a noun plural like -s in English, but only used when meaning needs clarifying or for emphasis | 학생들 *haksaeng-tŭl* students |
| 만 -man | **"only"** | 맥주만 *maekchu-man* only beer |

Note that Korean does not have any equivalent of the English articles **a** and **the**.

Pronouns
Because word dropping is common in Korean (see above), pronouns can often be omitted. Indeed, this is one part of the Korean language that is not particularly developed.

First person pronouns (I/we)
저 *chŏ* and 나 *na*
저 *chŏ* is more polite than 나 *na* and is used when talking to people older or superior to you and to strangers

Second person pronouns (you)
Korean has no universal polite second person pronoun. When addressing close friends of similar age 너 *nŏ* is used. Otherwise, you should either use the person's name or title. If you are unsure how to address an elder or superior, try using 선생님 *sŏnsaengnim*, which literally means "teacher" but can be used as a term of respect to more or less anyone.

Third person pronouns (he/she/it/they)
Korean has no third person pronoun as such. However, it is possible to use expressions such as 그 선생님 *kŭ sŏnsaengnim* ("that teacher", although it can be used as a respectful term for non-teachers as well), 그 친구 *kŭ ch'ingu* (that friend), 그 남자 *kŭ namja* (that man), 그 여자 *kŭ yŏja* (that woman), 그 사람 *kŭ saram* (that person), 그 분 (that person – respectful), etc.

For inanimate objects, you can use the expression 그 거 *kŭ kŏ* (that thing).

There is/there are/I have

있어요 *issŏyo* and 없어요 *ŏpsŏyo* are two very useful words to know. The former translates as "there is"/"there are" or "I have"/"you have"/"he/she/it has". The latter is the equivalent of "there isn't"/"there aren't" or "I don't have"/"you don't have"/"he/she/it doesn't have"

> 김치가 있어요? *kimch'i-ga issŏyo?*
> is there any kimchi? *or* do you have any kimchi?
> 아니요, 김치가 없어요 *aniyo, kimch'i-ga ŏpsŏyo*
> no, there isn't any kimchi *or* no, we don't have any kimchi

있어요 *issŏyo* and 없어요 *ŏpsŏyo* are also used when talking about the location of people or things:

> 민호가 서점에 있어요 *Min-ho-ga sŏjŏm-e issŏyo*
> Min-ho is at the bookstore

To be

In most cases, "be" translates into Korean as ―이에요 *-ieyo*. The corresponding negative expression is 아니에요 *anieyo*. Note that whereas *-ieyo* must always attach directly onto a noun, *anieyo* appears as an independent word.

> 학생이에요? *haksaeng-ieyo* are you a student?
> 아니요, 학생 아니에요 *aniyo, haksaeng anieyo* no, I'm not a student
> 회사원이에요 *hwesawon-ieyo* I'm an office worker

Verbs and verb endings

Korean is rich with verb endings that express tense, mood and many other functions. Note that unlike languages such as French, Korean verb endings do NOT change depending on grammatical person (I, you, he, she, we, they).

(a) Speech styles

Korean speakers attach different endings onto the verb stem depending on whom you are talking to and how formal the occasion is. The same sentence "(I) go" may be said (with the pronoun dropped) as 가 *ka* when talking with your friend, 가요 *kayo* when talking with your boss and 갑니다 *kamnida* when making a speech. Confusing? Yes, it can be, but to make things easier, in this book almost all sentences are given in the 가요 *kayo* style. This style is polite enough to be used in all but the most formal of occasions. Also, you can usually obtain the more intimate 가 *ka* style simply by dropping the — 요 *-yo* off the end. Be warned that this can be extremely offensive unless the other person is a close friend of similar age.

The other advantage of the 가요 *kayo* style is that the ending does not change depending on whether you are making a statement, asking a question (어디 가요? *ŏdi kayo?* where are you going?) or ordering someone to do something (빨리 가요! *ppalli kayo!* go quickly!). However, there are ways to make such questions and commands more polite (see below).

(b) Honorifics in polite questions and commands

When asking questions where "you" would be the grammatical subject and when ordering someone to do something, it is more polite to use a special honorific verb ending -*(ŭ)seyo*.

Thus, instead of asking 어디 가요? *ŏdi kayo?* where are you going? (as above), it would be more polite to say 어디 가세요? *ŏdi kaseyo?* 빨리 가요! *ppalli kayo!* go quickly! would also sound better than 빨리 가세요! *ppalli kaseyo!*

(c) Tenses

To put a sentence into the past tense, the —었/—았 *-ŏss/-ass* pre-final verb ending is added. "Min-ho went" thus becomes 민호가 갔어요 *Min-ho-ga kassŏyo*.

To form the future tense, the easiest and most universal way is to add the ending —을 거에요 *-(ŭ)l kŏ-eyo*. "Min-ho will go" thus becomes 민호가 갈 거에요 *Min-ho-ga kal kŏ-eyo*.

(d) A few modal expressions

Most modal expressions (expressions of volition, obligation, ability, etc) are formed by attaching another word or words onto the stem of the main verb.

"I want to (do something)"

Add –고 싶어요 -ko ship'ŏyo to the main verb:

김치를 먹고 싶어요 kimch'i-rŭl mokko ship'ŏyo I want to eat kimchi

"I can"

Add –을 수 있어요 -(ŭ)l su issŏyo to the main verb

내일 갈 수 있어요 naeil kal su issŏyo I can go tomorrow

"I can't"

Add –을 수 없어요 -(ŭ)l su ŏpsŏyo to the main verb

화요일에 갈 수 없어요 hwayoil-e kal su ŏpsŏyo I can't go on Tuesday

Alternatively, and especially when you are talking about a specific ability, you can just put 못 mot in front of the verb.

일본말을 못 해요 ilbon-mal-ŭl mot haeyo I can't speak Japanese

"You have to"

Add –(어/아)야 돼요 -(ŏ/a)ya twaeyo to the main verb.

9시까지 가야 돼요 ahop-shi-kkaji kaya twaeyo I have to go by nine o'clock

"You may"

Add –(어/아)도 돼요 -(ŏ/a)do twaeyo to the main verb.

여기서 담배를 피워도 돼요 yŏgi-sŏ tambae-rŭl p'iwo-do twaeyo you may smoke here

"You may/must not"

Add –(으)면 안 돼요 -(ŭmy)ŏn an twaeyo to the main verb

여기서 사진 찍으면 안 돼요 yŏgi-sŏ sajin tchik-ŭmyŏn an twaeyo you must not take photographs here

Negatives

Confusingly, there are as many as three ways to make a sentence negative in Korean. As can be seen in the examples below, the first two involve inserting the words 못 *mot* or 안 *an* before the main verb. The third involves adding —지 않아요 *-ji anayo* at the end of the verb:

학교에 못 가요 *hakkyo-e mot kayo* I can't go to school
학교에 안 가요 *hakkyo-e an kayo* I'm not going to school
학교에 가지 않아요 *hakkyo-e kaji anayo* I'm not going to school

There is a difference in meaning between the first of these expressions and the other two. 못 *mot* emphasizes an inability to do something due to reasons outside the speaker's control.

Adjectives

The main characteristic of Korean adjectives is that their structure and behaviour is almost identical to verbs. Adjectives are therefore freestanding – they do not need to be used with the verb "to be" as in English sentences such as "Su-mi *is* pretty". In Korean, this sentence can just be expressed as

수미가 예뻐요 *Su-mi-ga yeppŏyo*, literally "Su-mi pretty".

Adverbs

Adverbs can be formed by adding —게 *-ke* to the verb stem. For example, 예쁘게 *yeppŭge* means "prettily" in the following sentence:

수미가 예쁘게 웃었어요 *Su-mi-ga yeppŭge usŏssŏyo* Su-mi laughed prettily

However, Korean has many adverbs that are not formed in this way and have to be treated as separate words.

Asking questions

who?	누구 *nugu*
what?	뭐 *mŏ*
when?	언제 *ŏnje*
where?	어디 *ŏdi*
how?	어떻게 *ŏttŏk'e*
which?	어느 *ŏnŭ*
what kind of?	무슨 *musŭn*

HOLIDAYS AND FESTIVALS

The two most important holidays in Korea are 설날 *sŏlnal* (Lunar New Year) and 추석 *ch'usŏk* (Harvest Festival). These are family celebrations at which Koreans visit their parents or other relatives and pay their respects to deceased ancestors. For the vast numbers of South Koreans who have moved to the Seoul area from the countryside, this involves a mass pilgrimage from the capital to their ancestral homes. Expect transport chaos at these times, with road journeys often taking two or three times longer than usual.

For 설날 *sŏlnal* and 추석 *ch'usŏk*, the South Korean government commonly grants two or three consecutive days of public holiday. Note that for other public holidays, the holiday is always observed on that exact date, regardless of what day of the week this falls on. Many Koreans work a six-day week from Monday to Saturday and curse their luck when a holiday fall on a Sunday and is thus "lost" as an extra day off work!

Public holidays (South Korea)

1 January	신정 *shinjŏng* New Year
1st day, 1st month (lunar calendar)	설날 *sŏlnal* Lunar New Year
1 March	3.1절 *samiljŏl* "1 March holiday"; Independence Movement Day (to commemorate the 1919 uprising against Japanese occupation)
5 May	어린이날 *orininal* Children's Day
8th day, 4th month (lunar calendar)	부처님 오신 날 *puchŏnim oshin nal* Buddha's Birthday
6 June	현충일 *hyŏnch'ungil* Memorial Day
17 July	제헌절 *chehŏnjŏl* Constitution Day (to commemorate the founding of the first constitution of the Republic of Korea in 1948)
15 August	광복절 *kwangbokchŏl* Liberation Day (to commemorate liberation from Japanese imperial rule in 1945)
15th day, 8th month (lunar calendar)	추석 *ch'usŏk* Harvest Festival
3 October	개천절 *kaech'ŏnjŏl* National

Foundation Day (to celebrate the ancient founding of the Korean nation and the myth of 단군 *Tangun sŏngt'anjŏl* Christmas Day

25 December 성탄절

Festivals (South Korea)

New Year (신정 *shinjŏng*)
For the Korean version of New Year celebrations, make your way down to 종로 *Jeongro* in Seoul for fun with firecrackers and the ringing of the bell at the 종각 *Jonggak* pavilion.

Lunar New Year (설날 *sŏlnal*)
Koreans visit their home towns and feast on steaming bowls of 떡국 *ttŏkkuk* (rice-cake soup).

Valentine's Day (발렌타인 데이 *pallentin tei*)
In a custom imported from Japan, women give gifts to men on Valentine's day whereas men give gifts to women one month later on 14 March, which is called "White Day" (화이트 데이 *hwait'ŭ tei*). In a Korean twist, the day one month on from this (14 April) has been labelled "Black day" (블랙 데이 *pŭllaek tei*) and set aside for any remaining singles to meet up and eat 짜장면 *tchajangmyŏn* – black bean noodles!

Arbour Day (식목일 *shingmokil*)
5 April is national plant-a-tree day! This day originated in post-war Korea and attempts by the government to reforest the country devastated by war. Arbour day is no longer a public holiday.

Children's Day (어린이날 *orininal*)
This is a day for parents to treat their children to a fun day out. Expect amusement parks, zoos and so on to be teeming on this day!

Parents' Day (어버이날 *ŏbŏinal*)
Celebrated on 8 May, this is Mother's Day and Father's Day rolled into one!

Buddha's Birthday (부처님 오신 날 *puchŏnim oshin nal*)
This is a time when Buddhists visit temples and light colourful prayer lanterns.

Dano Festival (단오 *tano*)
This is a day of festivals and merrymaking to mark the start of summer,

which is most observed in rural Korea. It falls on the 5th day of the 5th lunar month.

Harvest Festival (추석 *ch'usŏk*)
As well as celebrating the harvest, this is also the day on which Koreans pay respects to deceased ancestors in a ceremony called 차례 *ch'are*.

Christmas Day (성탄절 *sŏngt'anjŏl*)
Some may be surprised to hear that over a quarter of South Koreans are Christian. For the younger generation, Christmas Day is also thought of as a romantic day to go out on a date with one's boyfriend or girlfriend.

USEFUL ADDRESSES

IN THE UK:

Embassy of The Republic of Korea (South Korea)
60 Buckingham Gate, London SW1E 6AJ
Tel: 020 7227 5500
Fax: 020 7227 5503
Website: korea.embassyhomepage.com

Embassy of The Democratic Peoples Republic of Korea (North Korea)
73 Gunnersbury Avenue, London W5 4LP
Tel: 020 8992 4965
Fax: 020 8992 2653

KTO (Korea Tourism Organization), London office
3rd floor, New Zealand House, Haymarket, London SW1Y 4TE
Tel: 0207 321 2535
Fax: 0207 321 0876
E-mail: london@mail.knto.or.kr
Website: www.tour2korea.com

SOAS Language Centre (Korean language classes)
School of Oriental and African Studies, Thornhaugh Street, Russell Square,
London WC1H 0XG
Tel: 020 7898 4888
Fax: 020 7898 4889
E-mail: languages@soas.ac.uk
Website: www.soas.ac.uk/languagecentre

IN THE US:

Embassy of The Republic of Korea (South Korea)
2450 Massachusetts Avenue, NW, Washington, DC 20008
Tel: 202 939 5600
Website: www.koreaembassyusa.org/

KTO (Korea Tourism Organization), NJ office
1 Executive Drive, Suite 100, Fort Lee, NJ 07024
Tel: 201 585 0909
E-mail: ny@kntoamerica.com
Website: www.tour2korea.com

IN SOUTH KOREA
British Embassy, Seoul
Taepyungro 40, 4 Jeong-dong, Jung-gu, Seoul 100-120
Tel: 02 3210 5500
E-mail: bembassy@uk.or.kr
Website: follow links from www.britishembassy.gov.uk

US Embassy, Seoul
32 Sejongno, Jongno-gu, Seoul 110-710
Tel: 02 397 4114
Fax: 02 397 4101
E-mail: seoul_acs@state.gov
Website: seoul.usembassy.gov

IN NORTH KOREA
British Embassy, Pyongyang
Munsu-dong Diplomatic Compound, Pyongyang
Tel: 02 382 7980
Fax: 02 381 7985
E-mail: postmaster.PYONX@fco.gov.uk
Website: follow links from www.fco.gov.uk

Website of KTO (Korea Tourism Organization):
www.tour2korea.com

Website of Koryo Tours, Beijing-based company specializing in travel to
North Korea:
www.koryogroup.com

Website of Sogang University, offering online Korean lessons:
korean.sogang.ac.kr/

CONVERSION TABLES

MEASUREMENTS

The metric system is used in Korea, except for one or two exceptions (see clothes sizes).

Length
1 cm ≈ 0.4 inches
30 cm ≈ 1 foot

Distance
1 metre ≈ 1 yard
1 km ≈ 0.6 miles

To convert kilometres into miles, divide by 8 and then multiply by 5.

kilometres	1	2	5	10	20	100
miles	0.6	1.25	3.1	6.25	12.50	62.5

To convert miles into kilometres, divide by 5 and then multiply by 8.

miles	1	2	5	10	20	100
kilometres	1.6	3.2	8	16	32	160

Weight

25g ≈ 1 oz   1 kg ≈ 2 lb   6 kg ≈ 1 stone

To convert kilos into pounds, divide by 5 and then multiply by 11.
To convert pounds into kilos, multiply by 5 and then divide by 11.

kilos	1	2	10	20	60	80
pounds	2.2	4.4	22	44	132	176

Liquid

1 litre ≈ 2 pints
4.5 litres ≈ 1 gallon

Temperature

To convert temperatures in Fahrenheit into Celsius, subtract 32, multiply by

5 and then divide by 9.
To convert temperatures in Celsius into Fahrenheit, divide by 5, multiply by 9 and then add 32.

Fahrenheit (°F)	32	40	50	59	68	86	100
Celsius (°C)	0	4	10	15	20	30	38

CLOTHES SIZES

Sometimes you will find sizes given using the English-language abbreviations **XS** (Extra Small), **S** (Small), **M** (Medium), **L** (Large) and **XL** (Extra Large). However, note that these sizes will generally be less generous than the equivalent back home!

Otherwise, you will find Korean clothing sizes to be a confusing mixture of imperial measurements (trousers, collars), metric measurements (bras, chest, shoes) and other numbers (women's clothes)!

- **Women's clothes**

Korea	55	66	77	88	99	etc
UK	8	10	12	14	16	

- **Bras**

Korea	70	75	80	85	90	etc
UK	32	34	36	38	40	

- **Men's shirts (collar size)**

Shirt collar sizes are quoted in inches, as in the UK. Some men, however, complain that Korean inches are somehow smaller than UK inches!

- **Trousers (men and women)**

Trouser sizes are measured in inches. However, again some people find that these sizes are somehow smaller than back home!

- **Tops (men and women)**

The size of tops are often quoted according to the chest measurement in centimetres. For women, 80 is considered extra small, 85 is small, 90 is medium and 100 is large. For men, 90 is considered small, 95 is medium, 100 is large and 105 is extra large. Again, these ideas of small, medium and large may be less generous than those in the UK.

Shoe sizes

Shoe sizes are given in millimetres and increase in increments of 5 millimetres.

- **Women's shoes**

Korea	235	240	250	255	265	etc
UK	4	5	6	7	8	

- **Men's shoes**

Korea	255	260	265	275	280	etc
UK 7	8	9	10	11		